Professional Image

Professional Development Series

Author:

Ann A. Cooper, M.Ed.
Central Carolina Technical College
Sumter, South Carolina

SOUTH-WESTERN
THOMSON LEARNING

Australia • Canada • Mexico • Singapore • Spain • United Kingdom • United States

SOUTH-WESTERN
★
™
THOMSON LEARNING

Professional Image
By Ann Cooper

Vice President/Editor-in-Chief
Jack Calhoun

Executive Marketing Manager:
Carol Volz

Copy Editor:
Marianne Miller

Vice President/Executive Publisher:
Dave Shaut

Marketing Manager:
Chris McNamee

Compositor:
Electro-Publishing

Team Leader:
Karen Schmohe

Marketing Coordinator:
Cira Brown

Printer:
Edwards Bros./Ann Arbor

Project Manager:
Dr. Inell Bolls

Manufacturing Manager:
Charlene Taylor

Rights and Permissions Manager:
Linda Ellis

Production Editor:
Carol Spencer

Design Project Manager:
Stacy Jenkins Shirley

Production Manager:
Tricia Boies

Cover and Internal Design:
Grannan Graphic Design, Ltd.

For more information, contact
South-Western
5191 Natorp Boulevard
Mason, OH 45040
Or, visit our Internet site at
www.swlearning.com.

For permission to use material from this text or product, contact us by
Phone: 1-800-730-2214,
Fax: 1-800-730-2215, or
www.thomsonrights.com.

Gain the Insight to Professional Success

Keeping pace with today's competitive marketplace is a challenge.

Although technology has enabled us to communicate and produce in ways we never thought possible, there are other essential elements to achieving professional success. *The Professional Development Series* is a quick and practical resource for learning non-technical strategies and tactics.

0-538-72463-3	Business Etiquette & Protocol
0-538-72527-3	Customer Relations & Rapport
0-538-72484-6	Leadership in Organizations
0-538-72474-9	Career Planning & Networking
0-538-72485-4	Team Dynamics

The 10-Hour Series

This series enables you to become proficient in a variety of technical skills in only a short amount of time through ten quick and easy lessons.

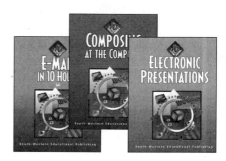

0-538-69458-0	E-mail in 10 Hours
0-538-68928-5	Composing at the Computer
0-538-69849-7	Electronic Business Presentations

Quick Skills Series

Quickly sharpen the interpersonal skills you need for job success and professional development with the Quick Skills Series. This series features career-related scenarios for relevant and real application of skills.

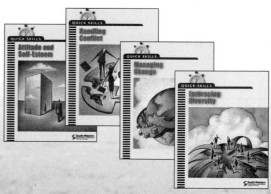

0-538-69026-7	Attitude and Self Esteem
0-538-69833-0	Handling Conflict
0-538-69839-X	Managing Change
0-538-69842-X	Embracing Diversity

SOUTH-WESTERN
_____
THOMSON LEARNING

Join us on the Internet
www.swep.com

Contents

Preface

The professional image projected by an individual in the business environment is very important and can have a profound effect on the career advancement of the individual. Professional image involves both the appearance and the behavior of an individual in the business world. Professional image is a complex issue that requires focus on detail and attention to an overall goal. An individual can effectively develop both appearance and behavior through management of his or her professional image. This *Professional Image* module provides a practical guide to the identification of appropriate techniques for the development of a positive professional image.

Message to the User

Professional Image is organized into eight topics for easy reference. These topics provide an overview of the different aspects of professional image development. The module is designed to serve as a reference guide in helping you identify the components of a professional image. It also provides steps and techniques for accomplishing your professional image goals. The following is a brief overview of each topic:

Professional Image

Discusses the definition of a professional image and the attributes of a professional.

Professional Appearance

Identifies the attributes of professional appearance from appropriate grooming to health habits and nutrition.

Professional Dress

Defines professional dress and the significance of dress in the business environment. Includes helpful techniques for both men and women.

Wardrobe Management

Discusses the importance of identifying individual style and techniques for building a professional wardrobe.

Manners and Etiquette for the Professional

Presents the importance of manners and etiquette in the business environment. Includes tips on introductions, dining, and gift giving.

Personal Behavior

Discusses the responsibilities associated with personal behavior, an important aspect of professional image.

Communicating Professionally

Presents effective communication techniques, which include speaking, writing, and listening skills.

Professional Image Development

Presents the resources available for the development of a professional image.

Features

Each topic begins with clear goals entitled "At the Core." A list of key concepts is presented at the end of each topic. A pre- and post-assessment activity is also included at the beginning and end of the module, which may be used as a fun, non-graded activity. *Professional Image* is organized into eight topics summarized previously. Case studies are provided at the end of the module to engage the user in critical thinking. Online resources for further research on every topic are also provided at the end of the module.

About the Author

Ann A. Cooper has over 25 years of experience in the field of business and education. Her teaching experience includes primarily post secondary business education. Ann presently serves in a leadership role as vice president for Academic and Student Affairs at Central Carolina Technical College in Sumter, South Carolina. She has worked as a private consultant and has served as a speaker in business education at national, regional, and state conferences. Ann is involved in a variety of leadership positions in professional and civic organizations. She served as president of the South Carolina Business Education Association and as president of the Southern Business Education Association. She was a member of the National Business Education Executive Board. She is vice chairman of the Lee County Economic Alliance and is the first woman to serve in this capacity. Ann has been recognized for her leadership expertise by her peers and has received various awards for leadership and distinguished service to her profession. Ann received her undergraduate degree from Winthrop University and her masters degree from the University of South Carolina.

Pre-Assessment Activity

Directions: Read each of the following statements and questions carefully. Circle the letter of the best response.

1. Which of the following are attributes of a professional image?
   a. professional appearance
   b. use of manners and etiquette
   c. appropriate personal behavior
   d. effective communications
   e. all of the above

2. Being aware of which section of the country in which you reside as it relates to your professional dress means you are making decisions about your appearance based on which of the following criteria?
   a. types of functions you must attend
   b. geographic location
   c. budget and purchasing techniques
   d. clothing care and maintenance
   e. profession

3. A first impression is usually made within what time frame?
   a. 5 to 30 seconds
   b. 10 minutes
   c. after 15 minutes
   d. 30 minutes
   e. 1 hour

4. What is the major personal benefit of having a positive professional image?
   a. developing better friends
   b. being an effective communicator
   c. having a heightened sense of self-confidence
   d. having positive performance appraisals
   e. earning a better salary

5. What is an element of a healthy lifestyle as it relates to professional image?
   a. nutrition
   b. exercise
   c. diet
   d. regular visits to a physician
   e. all of the above

6. Characteristics of professional dress include:
   a. comfortable and casual
   b. comfortable and a proper fit
   c. well-maintained and clean
   d. appropriate for all occasions
   e. both b and c

7. What concept related to professional dress has developed over the past decade?
   a. company policies regarding dress
   b. uniforms for employees
   c. casual dress day
   d. customer profiling regarding dress
   e. none of the above

8. What color of a basic suit is best for the male professional?
   a. beige or khaki
   b. dark basic color such as charcoal gray
   c. navy blue
   d. black
   e. burgundy

9. What is the most powerful item of clothing for female professionals?
   a. skirted suit
   b. business dress
   c. jacket
   d. pantsuit
   e. briefcase

10. Lines that accentuate the body can be created by:
    a. a seam
    b. a hem
    c. color
    d. the end of a garment
    e. all of the above

11. How far below the hem of the sleeve of a suit jacket should a man's shirt sleeve extend?
    a. not at all
    b. one-half to three-quarters of an inch
    c. one inch
    d. less than one-quarter of an inch
    e. more than one inch

12. Hosiery should match which item for a woman?
    a. jacket
    b. skirt
    c. shoes
    d. blouse
    e. all of the above

13. What is the primary accessory for the male professional?
    a. tie
    b. belt
    c. shoes
    d. jewelry
    e. socks

14. Being respectful of another person's background and ethnicity is related to what concept?
    a. manners
    b. etiquette
    c. cultural diversity
    d. appreciation
    e. protocol

15. When introducing people, what is a good general rule to remember?
    a. make introductions during the first 15 seconds of people meeting
    b. mention first the name of the person you want to honor
    c. give a short introduction about the person prior to providing names
    d. let others introduce themselves
    e. ask if the people in the group know each other

16. When should you place your napkin in your lap at dinner in a restaurant?
    a. as soon as you are seated
    b. after the server takes drink orders
    c. prior to the first course
    d. when the salad is served
    e. when the host places the napkin in his or her lap

17. What should be the objective of giving a gift to someone who has extended a kindness to you?
    a. to show that you appreciate his or her kindness
    b. to demonstrate your good taste in gift selection
    c. to maintain a friendship
    d. to avoid any obligation on your part
    e. all of the above

18. Which characteristic is demonstrated by doing your job correctly in a timely manner without someone telling you to do it?
    a. initiative
    b. honesty
    c. integrity
    d. responsibility
    e. trustworthiness

19. What is one of the most difficult changes for professionals to accept?
    a. dress codes in their profession
    b. organizational structure in their company
    c. job relocations
    d. new policies
    e. performance appraisals

20. What type of communication is offensive to some people and difficult to understand?
    a. slang
    b. cursing
    c. acronyms
    d. jargon
    e. all of the above

1
Professional Image

AT THE CORE
This topic examines:

➤ **THE CONCEPT OF A PROFESSIONAL IMAGE**

➤ **ATTRIBUTES OF A PROFESSIONAL IMAGE**

➤ **THE IMPORTANCE AND SIGNIFICANCE OF A PROFESSIONAL IMAGE**

➤ **THE EFFECTS OF A PROFESSIONAL IMAGE ON SELF-CONFIDENCE**

➤ **DEVELOPMENT OF A PROFESSIONAL IMAGE**

t may seem somewhat unfair to judge an individual by appearance and behavior rather than exclusively on performance; but in most business environments, judgments are made about people based on the professional image they display as a result of appearance and behavior. This occurs before the individual's level of competence or performance is determined. Judgments are made about people both internal and external to the organization as they interact with people. Consequently, the significance of professional image can be substantial in the business world, and you should be aware of this as you develop your personal standards for appearance and behavior.

> *"Nothing succeeds like the appearance of success."*
> **—Christopher Leach**

Although some standards of appearance for professional dress have changed over the last decade, certain expectations remain for appropriate and professional appearance in the business environment. The business world is still more conservative than liberal in its regard for professionalism. You should seize the opportunity to distinguish yourself positively in a sometimes lax environment by adopting high standards in your professional appearance. This could be a significant factor in your career advancement.

©PhotoDisc

In the business environment, you must understand what constitutes a professional image in order to effectively meet the standards and expectations you set for yourself. In addition, you must recognize the importance of a professional image and how this affects self-confidence; interaction with peers, customers, and supervisors; and ultimate success in your career mobility. Professional image can be viewed from two major perspectives: appearance and personal behavior. In the area of appearance, you want to develop your ability to dress appropriately and present yourself in an attractive manner. In the area of personal behavior, you want to develop your communication skills and your finesse in the use of proper manners and etiquette as well as recognize the importance of appropriate personal behavior. Finally, you should identify resources for image development so you are aware of and can maintain a professional image throughout your career.

> *"Looking the part helps get you the chance to fill it."*
> **—Macolm Forbes**

The Concept of a Professional Image

Exactly what is a professional image? Is it how you dress? Your grooming? The quality or cost of your clothing? What creates an individual's professional image? "Your professional image is the image you project in the professional business world."[1] A professional image is an overall concept that is a composite of many aspects of your appearance.

Professional image consists of personal appearance with regard to clothing, grooming, manners and etiquette, personal behavior, and communication effectiveness.

Attributes of a Professional Image

The four main attributes of a professional image include:

- Appropriate professional appearance.
- Use of correct manners and etiquette.
- Appropriate personal behavior.
- Effective communications.

Each of these attributes has many aspects in your achieving the overall appropriate and positive image you desire. It is important to pay attention to detail and to remember at all times that your professional image is a composite of both your appearance and your behavior.

Appropriate Professional Appearance. Professional appearance is a composite of your professional dress and your grooming. The message communicated is a result of the combination of these two factors. Professional dress can be defined as dressing in such a manner as to enhance your authority, promote your respect, aid in your promotion, and promote your advancement opportunities in the workplace. Professional dress involves appropriate clothing selection based on the following considerations:

- Profession
- Company policies
- Level of customer and client interaction
- Geographic location
- Clothing care and maintenance
- Appropriate styles for your individual body
- Types of functions you must attend
- Budget and purchasing techniques

Each of these will be presented in greater detail later in this module; however, you can see from the list that achieving an appropriate professional appearance requires time and careful thought in the achievement of the desired result.

Personal grooming habits are also very important in your professional image. You must develop and practice good grooming habits to ensure that your appearance is clean and polished in your professional role. Grooming involves all aspects of your body, including the following:

- Overall cleanliness
- Hair
- Nails
- Teeth
- Makeup

Manners and Etiquette. Your professional image is also communicated through your use of appropriate manners and etiquette. You should be familiar with the different protocols of behavior as they relate to social manners and etiquette. Some of these include:

- Making introductions and appropriate greetings.
- Being able to initiate and maintain conversations.
- Respecting the customs of others.
- Being able to express appreciation.
- Knowing appropriate dining rules and protocol.
- Extending courteous behavior to others.
- Knowing how to behave in difficult situations.

Manners and etiquette are important in the overall professional image you project. You can learn to be proficient in these areas and enhance your professional image with practice and attention in determining the etiquette requirements for different situations.

Most people feel comfortable once they are sure about what is expected and know how to carry out these expectations. Many resources are available to help you develop this aspect of your professional image.

TIP   Your personal behavior also communicates a message about your professional image.

Personal Behavior. As a professional, you want to practice a code of personal behavior that demonstrates respect for your organization and the people who work with you. You should recognize that personal behavior contributes to the overall professional image you project. Some aspects of personal behavior include:

©Digital Stock

- Respecting the organization and its rules.
- Being a loyal employee.
- Conducting business in an ethical manner.
- Assuming responsibility.
- Respecting the diversity of people.

Each of these aspects of personal behavior is very important in the business world, and your reputation for being committed to them will be established early in your career. You should give careful attention to personal behavior. Many people have been high achievers who projected an appropriate image in their appearance and yet failed in their career because they did not take responsibility for their personal behavior.

Communications. Another significant component of your professional image is your ability to communicate effectively with others. Communication should be clear, concise, and accurate. You communicate nonverbally as well as verbally in the business world. Nonverbal communications send messages about your professional image. These nonverbal communications include the following:

- Posture
- Facial gestures
- Neatness
- Listening
- Personal behavior
- Punctuality

For example, a person who is usually late may not say "I don't respect your time," but that is certainly the message that is communicated through this nonverbal action.

In addition to nonverbal communications, your overall ability to communicate effectively is very important. Effective communications required in the business environment include the following:

- Speaking correctly.
- Writing appropriate communications.
- Expressing written appreciation.
- Listening effectively.
- Communicating verbally in difficult situations.

Communication abilities can be developed and refined as you progress through your career. It is important to give significant attention to the development of these skills as they not only contribute to your professional image but also may determine the level of advancement you attain in your career.

> **TIP** The ability to communicate effectively is a major attribute of a positive professional image.

The Importance and Significance of a Professional Image

The importance and significance of a professional image should not be underestimated. "The way you look may not make up for poor performance, but it could give you a competitive edge during your interview and in your future career. Employers often decide whether an applicant will fit in with their organization based on a first impression."[2] This statement reflects the importance of a professional image in the business world. The effect on your career can be significant and varied and may include:

- Selection for participation on project teams.
- Inclusion in social settings with customers or clients.
- Selection for presentations.
- Promotions to positions of greater responsibility.
- Performance rating.
- Overall competitiveness in numerous situations.

"Some of the perceptions people can form solely from your appearance are professionalism, level of sophistication, intelligence, and credibility. Whether these perceptions are real or imagined, they underscore how your appearance instantly influences the opinions of strangers, colleagues, and superiors. The benefits of being well dressed in a corporate setting can reap many rewards, including respect, and, all things considered, promotions."[3]

©PhotoDisc, Inc.

The significance of a professional image may seem unfair, but it is a real and substantial factor in the business world nonetheless. You may find many issues to be less than fair, but they do indeed exist in the business world. Most business environments have expectations for the professional image of their employees; this alone should indicate to you the importance of image, as it will impact opportunities for your advancement in the business world. You should consider your professional image as a significant "communicator" to others. Success in the business world is usually a result of job knowledge, human relations abilities, and professional image. Most people want to communicate to their peers, supervisors, and customers that they are ready for business, they are prepared for their role, and they possess the competence to perform their job. Your professional image does all of this.

The Effects of a Professional Image on Self-Confidence

The effect of a professional image on your career and your interaction with others can be significant. Your professional image not only affects how others react and interact with you but also affects your self-confidence and performance. When you believe you are dressed appropriately, know the required protocol, and are comfortable communicating with others, you tend to feel a heightened sense of self-confidence because you know what to do and how to do it. This sense of self-confidence can positively influence your performance. In addition to your increased self-confidence, others around you perceive your professionalism in a positive manner and, consequently, believe you are able to perform your job in a satisfactory manner.

Gaining the Respect of Others. You also gain the respect of others by projecting a positive professional image. This respect is important, as people observe you and form opinions about your professional image. Many times throughout the course of a day's work you will be observed and evaluated in an informal manner. These observations contribute to the overall perception that people have about you. Supervisors and peers make judgments, choices, and decisions based on these observations over a period of time.

> **TIP**   You only have one opportunity to make a first impression.

First Impressions. In initial job interviews, judgments are made on your professional image, your manners, and your communication abilities. These judgments result in decisions about whether you are the best candidate for a position. The importance of professional image as it relates to first impressions and career mobility is significant and should be considered at all times. You only have one opportunity to make a good first impression. Take this opportunity seriously, and concentrate on making a positive first impression. "Your image can smooth your way or stop you cold. With great effort, you can usually overcome a bad first impression, but why waste the time? Start right, start strong, and your image will be your most powerful advocate, telling people who and what you are as you connect with them and get your message across."[4]

Development of a Professional Image

Given the many aspects of a professional image, you may wonder where you can learn about professional image and find answers to questions that may be difficult or embarrassing to ask others. Many resources are available to enhance both your knowledge and performance in developing a professional image. Some resources include the following:

- Literature
- Online resources

- Consultants
- Mentors and role models
- Training and professional development opportunities
- Company policies and procedures

Each of these can assist you in developing a professional image, and each one has unique advantages over the other. Most professionals have used these resources at one time or another to create their desired professional image. You may use the Pre-Assessment Activity at the beginning of this module to conduct an assessment of the areas you desire to improve with regard to your professional image knowledge base.

You should identify the resources that are most appropriate for your individual needs. However, the observation of others is one of the most powerful learning tools for a professional, and this is especially true in the area of professional image. Look around and see what other successful professionals are wearing, how they communicate, and what rules of etiquette they are following. This can provide valuable information as you seek to develop your professional image.

RECAP OF KEY CONCEPTS

- The business world makes judgments about you based on your professional image.
- The business world has certain expectations for appropriate and professional appearance in the business environment.
- Professional image consists of personal appearance as it relates to clothing, grooming, manners and etiquette, personal behavior, and communication effectiveness.
- Professional appearance is a composite of your professional dress and your grooming.
- Professional dress is dressing in such a manner as to enhance your authority, promote your respect, aid in your promotion, and promote your advancement opportunities in the workplace.

- Professional dress involves appropriate clothing selection based on profession, company policies, level of customer interaction, geographic location, clothing care and maintenance, appropriate styles, types of functions, and budgetary resources available.
- Personal grooming involves your hair, nails, teeth, and make-up.
- Use appropriate manners and etiquette for making introductions, maintaining conversations, respecting the customs of others, expressing appreciation, knowing appropriate dining rules, extending courteous behavior, and knowing how to behave in difficult situations.
- Personal behavior is an important part of the professional image you project.
- Nonverbal communications include posture, facial gestures, neatness, listening, personal behavior, and punctuality. Each of these contributes to professional image.
- Effective communication includes speaking correctly, writing, expressing appreciation, listening effectively, and communicating effectively in difficult situations.
- Your professional image can have a significant impact on your career. This can be demonstrated in your selection for participation in company activities, your promotion potential, and your performance ratings.
- Your professional image also affects your self-confidence and performance.
- Many resources are available to assist in the development of a professional image. These include literature, online resources, consultants, mentors and role models, training and professional development opportunities, and company policies and procedures.

2
Professional Appearance

AT THE CORE
This topic examines:

➤ **INDIVIDUAL BODY ATTRIBUTES**

➤ **GROOMING**

➤ **HAIRSTYLES**

➤ **NAIL PRESENTATION**

➤ **USE OF MAKEUP**

➤ **EXERCISE AND HEALTH HABITS**

➤ **NUTRITION**

➤ **HEALTH CARE ASSISTANCE**

A professional image begins with solid habits in grooming, exercise, health, and nutrition. These serve as the foundation for other elements of your personal image, including the selection of hairstyles, nails, and makeup. You should not make the mistake of focusing your professional image exclusively on the clothes you wear. In fact, a professional image is a result of a combination of many things. Your professional image involves the care of your body and the maintenance of positive health habits. Your image is also affected by how you feel as well as how you look.

TIP You want to look and feel good to help project a professional image.

A professional image is a total package of how you appear and behave. Your hair, nails, makeup, grooming habits, health habits, exercise, and nutrition affect your appearance. Each one of these makes a significant contribution to how you look and feel as you work each day in your profession. There are accepted standards in the workplace with regard to each of these elements of appearance, and it is important to identify and abide by these standards of acceptability.

Individual Body Attributes

It is important to assess yourself and your individual body attributes so you can make wise clothing selections and take care of yourself. Every person has a unique body shape, and it is important to know your body well. As a result, you will be able to select clothing that is attractive, choose colors that enhance your complexion, accent positive attributes, and de-emphasize characteristics you consider less attractive. It is also important to know the special needs of your body. For instance, you may be a person who needs at least eight hours of sleep each night to function effectively the next day, you may need to eat smaller but more frequent meals, or you may be able to function better during the morning hours than at night. It is important to have a keen sense of understanding about your individual body and its needs so you can make wise choices in your self-management. A person who knows himself or herself well is more confident and able to manage situations more effectively. This is important in the development of your professional image because it allows you to set yourself up for success in your appearance and your behavior.

> **TIP** Assess your body type and individual needs to help you determine what is best for you.

Grooming

The foundation for any professional image is appropriate grooming. Good grooming habits involve attention to a daily routine of good hygiene and cleaning.

Good grooming guidelines include the following:

- Bathe daily and always after exercising.
- Shampoo hair regularly to avoid an oily or dirty look.
- Brush teeth after each meal.
- Keep breath fresh by using mouthwash and breath mints.
- Floss teeth daily.

©PhotoDisc, Inc.

- Use deodorant each day immediately after bathing.
- Keep eyebrows plucked or trimmed neatly.
- Keep all nose, ear, and facial hair trimmed closely.
- Use moisturizing body lotions to keep skin soft and supple especially on hands and feet.
- Keep legs and underarms free of hair (women).
- Keep nails clean and neatly trimmed.

A solid routine should be established for regular body maintenance. The formation of good grooming habits will produce the foundation for the professional image you want to project. Grooming is where your professional image begins. You must take time for grooming, or your overall image will be compromised and will not be as effective as it could be. Many grooming products on the market can assist you. In addition, you will occasionally need the assistance of a professional. You should schedule regular visits to your dentist. You may even want to visit a salon for assistance with the shaping of your eyebrows or for professional hair removal. Using a professional in the maintenance of your personal grooming is an investment in your professional image.

TIP   Effective grooming takes time and a focus on good techniques to yield the desired results.

Hairstyles

Most professionals seek to identify a hairstyle that is not only attractive but also easy to maintain. This is applicable for both men and women in the business environment. In general, the business world accepts hairstyles that are well maintained, clean, neat, and conservative.

TIP   Select a hairstyle that is attractive and easy to maintain to achieve a professional image.

"If your professional style isn't easy-care and adaptable, you lose," says New York City stylist Julien Farel. "Hair is one of the most noticeable physical factors affecting others' opinions of us."[1] In the selection and maintenance of your hairstyle, be mindful of the following guidelines:

©PhotoDisc, Inc.

- Select a style that is attractive to your facial shape.
- Select a style that is relatively carefree.
- Maintain a style that is suitable for your hair type.
- Maintain the cut, as this is the foundation for an attractive style.
- Maintain your hair color.
- Wear hair in a neat, confined style.
- Keep hair clean and well conditioned.
- Choose hair accessories that compliment a professional image.
- Use hair products sparingly to avoid a stiff look.

The grooming of your hair is important. To maintain a professional image, you should plan regular visits to your hair stylist for maintenance and upkeep of your hair, which includes cutting, coloring, and conditioning. Your hairstyle will communicate poor grooming habits if your hair is in need of attention. If color is used, it must be maintained; therefore, you must make this a part of your grooming routine. If you do not possess the expertise to color your hair, don't! Getting your hair professionally colored is well worth the investment.

For men who choose to have facial hair, it should also be well-maintained, neat, and trimmed. Beards and mustaches are attractive on some men and should always be well-groomed. Some organizations have policies pertaining to facial hair for men, and it is important for you to review these policies if applicable. Facial hair requires attention and maintenance. If color is used, it should be maintained.

"Recently, wearing braided hairstyles has become quite popular among Black students, both male and female. While there is no absolute on wearing braids or dreads, caution should be exercised. If wearing braids is something you feel strongly about, you should be sure and do your research on the company's culture. This is where a good information interview with someone in your network can be very beneficial. Braids, especially on men, are still not an acceptable part of the dress code in the business world. The more conservative the work environment, the less acceptable braids will be. If you do decide to go with braids, have them done professionally and wear them in a neat bun and pulled to the back. Never wear them long or shoulder length."[2]

Nail Presentation

As a business professional, you constantly use your hands when interacting with people. Throughout the day, you probably shake hands with customers and peers, pass out business cards, distribute materials, and request signatures on papers. Each of these situations requires that you display your hands to others. Because your hands are important to a professional, you should pay close attention to your nails.

> TIP   Nails are a very visible aspect of your professional image and should receive attention in your grooming routine.

Both men and women should develop and practice meticulous grooming habits for their nails. Nails should always be well-trimmed, neat, and impeccably clean. Mary Spillane and Christine Sherlock, in *Color Me Beautiful's Looking Your Best*, recommend keeping nails short to medium in length and well maintained. The shape should follow the fingertip shape.[3] The maintenance of your nails should be a part of your regular grooming routine. Women who choose to wear nail polish must keep it maintained. If you are not proficient in giving yourself a manicure and/or pedicure, then you should use a neutral or clear shade or visit a professional nail technician. Chipped nail polish can be distracting, and it looks unprofessional. If you wear open-toed shoes during the summer months, you must pay extra attention to your toenails; apply clear or neutral polish. When choosing colors for nail polish, be sure to select colors that are appropriate for the business environment. Nail polish should compliment your clothing and overall appearance. The use of long acrylic nails is somewhat dated and not appropriate for most business settings.

Use of Makeup

For most women, makeup enhances and improves their overall facial appearance. Remember that the objective of wearing makeup is to enhance natural features and to achieve an overall natural and polished appearance. If your makeup appears too obvious, the professional image you want to achieve is lost. Specific guidelines for using makeup are included as follows:

- Prepare skin appropriately with moisturizers prior to applying makeup.
- Select a shade of foundation that is close to your natural skin tone.
- Select a foundation that contains sunscreen.
- Use a concealer to cover discolorations and/or blemishes.
- Blend makeup carefully to avoid looking as though you are wearing a mask.
- Apply sheer powder over foundation to give a finished look.
- Select soft shades for blush and eye shadow.
- Apply mascara lightly.
- Select a lipstick color that compliments your clothing and blush tones.
- Take care of skin on a daily basis by cleansing and moisturizing.

Foundation, Concealer, and Blush. Women should pay close attention to makeup application. Remember, the overall objective is a natural look. Neutral shades are usually best for the business world. It is always important to keep your profession in mind and know what is appropriate when applying makeup. If you work in New York in a fashion environment, more makeup may be acceptable. However, most professionals work in a more conservative work environment and should apply makeup accordingly. Concealer should be applied after a moisturizer and should match skin tone as much as possible. Concealer should be

©PhotoDisc, Inc.

used sparingly, as too much draws attention to the discoloration or blemish rather than diminishing its appearance. Foundation follows the concealer.

> **TIP** Skin requires daily cleansing and moisturizing to maintain a healthy look.

Most professional makeup artists recommend using a sponge to apply foundation. You want to blend from the center of the face to the hairline and along your jawline. You should pay careful attention that makeup is not mixed into the hair roots around your face or in your eyebrows.[4] Blush should be applied on the cheek in an upward motion to enhance the cheek area. Avoid using blush in a bold color or applying too much. The objective in using blush is to enhance the cheek area naturally with a subtle and natural shade.

Eye Shadow, Mascara, and Brow Pencils. When selecting eye shadow, you want to look for natural colors that enhance your eyes but do not draw attention because of the color or amount used. The natural colors of brown and taupe compliment most skin tones. Eye shadows with a powder base usually last longer and do not crease in the folds of your eyelids like a cream-based shadow. Mascara should be applied to your lashes to enhance their appearance and define them. You should apply one to two coats of mascara after you apply your eye shadow. You want to avoid putting on too much so you do not overdo this feature of your eyes. Unless you are in the fashion world, false eyelashes are not appropriate for the business environment. Another useful tool for enhancing the eye area is the brow pencil, which defines and shapes your eyebrows. You should select a color that is close to your natural hair color.[5] You want to avoid brows that are in stark contrast to your hair color or ones that are heavily colored with pencil. Remember, you are trying to achieve a natural look. You may want to invest in a trip to a beauty salon for the initial shaping of your brows. Most people can maintain their eyebrows once they have a good shape to follow. This is one area in which a professional can lend some assistance to your professional image.

Men should pay close attention to the maintenance of their eyebrows, keeping the eyebrows trimmed and neat at all times. This is usually part of the regular maintenance of a haircut with a professional hairdresser.

Lipsticks. Lip color is the finishing element of makeup. Lip color should be selected to enhance your overall facial makeup. Lip color brightens the face and helps its overall appearance. Your goal in selecting a lip color is to achieve a polished and finished look. Do not overdo the color or amount. The use of gloss should be minimal, as this can create a greasy look that is inappropriate for the business world. You should use a lip pencil to define your lips and then fill in with lipstick. Lipstick should be maintained throughout the day.

Fragrances. Another consideration of grooming is the use of fragrances for men and women. Fragrances are acceptable in the workplace for the professional but should always be understated and "light." If for any reason someone in your office or work environment is allergic to fragrances, you should immediately refrain from using them. Whatever fragrance you select, it should produce a fresh and light effect.

TIP   Avoid fragrances that are heavy or overpowering.

Makeup Storage. You should keep your makeup in a clean, dry location. Makeup that is old and out of date may contain bacteria; therefore, keep a few products that work effectively for you rather than so many that they become old and unusable. You should also have a few basic makeup products with you for retouches throughout the day. A sheer powder compact and lipstick are usually two essentials most women need to maintain their makeup. You should always apply make-up in the privacy of your office or the rest room. Do not put makeup on or touch up your existing makeup in public. This projects a poor professional image.

Exercise and Health Habits

As a professional, you will have many demands on you. Because of these demands, you may create an environment in which attention to exercise and good health habits are secondary. This creates stress on your body. The importance and benefits of exercise continue to be presented in a variety of medical publications, studies, and research. Some of the benefits of regular exercise include lower blood pressure, reduced cholesterol, and reduction in the onset of diabetes and heart disease, as well as the ability to handle stress more effectively. You should always see your physician before beginning an exercise program, especially if you suspect serious health conditions.

Studies have indicated that people who exercise regularly actually have a better outlook on life and experience less depression. Not only does exercise help your internal system of organs, but it improves your physical appearance and supports the maintenance of strong bones, muscle tone, and skin tone. Exercise does not need to be strenuous or done in a formal setting. If you enjoy competitive sports or vigorous exercise, take advantage of them. However, you can also reap the benefits of an exercise program through regular walking or biking. If you live in an area where a safe and accessible walking area is not readily available, you should consider investing in a treadmill or stationary bike.

TIP   Taking time to exercise can increase your sense of wellness.

"A successful exercise program needs to suit you, to be one you can really enjoy and carry out regularly."[6] The most important aspect of exercising is making it a part of your regular routine at least four times per week. Most experts recommend exercising a minimum of four times per week for at least 30 minutes each day. Walking is the overall "winner" in the exercise category. Walking requires very little equipment—just a good pair of walking shoes—and is not stressful on joints and muscles. Walking can help you lose weight, maintain your weight, and build up cardiovascular endurance. Walking is also a great opportunity to meet a friend or family member for some uninterrupted quality time and relaxation.

Other health habits you should develop include the following:

- See your doctor for a physical at least once a year.
- Schedule regular visits with your dentist every six months.
- Schedule preventive testing such as mammograms and prostate cancer screening.
- Maintain a healthy weight.
- Take all medications as prescribed.
- When ill, stay home from work to recover.
- Avoid overexposure to the sun, and use sunscreen regularly.
- Avoid all use of tobacco.
- Limit the use of alcohol.
- Get an appropriate amount of rest each night.

Good health habits contribute to your overall health and feeling of wellness. It is important to listen to your body. Whenever something does not seem right, see your physician immediately. Paying attention to health problems and preventive maintenance can improve your overall health status.

The importance of adequate rest cannot be overemphasized. Many people work longer hours each day and get only a few hours of sleep each night. As a professional, you need to recognize the importance of getting adequate rest and how this affects your ability to interact with others. You must be well-rested in order to concentrate and work effectively with people each day. You cannot project a professional image if you are tired and unable to concentrate.

Nutrition

Professionals recognize the importance of a good diet and its relationship to how they feel and perform in the business world. Maintaining healthy nutritional habits becomes increasingly challenging as the demands for your time increase and you prepare fewer nutritious meals at home. Therefore, you must know what foods are good for your health and performance and be mindful of their importance to your overall well-being and professional image. Healthful eating habits can help you maintain an appropriate body weight and ensure the energy and nutrition necessary for a busy professional. Your body needs a balance of many nutrients to maintain appropriate nutritional and energy levels. The body needs protein for body tissue; carbohydrates for energy; and fat for energy, insulation, and certain body functions. Vitamins and minerals are also necessary for the body.[7] The vitamins found in dairy products build teeth and bones, and minerals contribute to the functioning of many internal organs and systems. Good nutrition is usually the result of a well-balanced diet that includes many vegetables, fruits, and complex carbohydrates.

©PhotoDisc, Inc.

TIP   A moderate, balanced diet should be the goal for your nutritional needs.

Research shows that you should limit your intake of sugars, fats, and salt to avoid many of the diseases caused by excessive consumption of these foods. Good nutrition usually does not mean you need to eliminate a particular food; it means you should consume the majority of your food from the vegetable, fruit, and grain categories while limiting refined sugars, fats, and salt. If your physician suggests the elimination of any of these foods, you should certainly follow his or her orders. Moderation in food consumption and an exercise program usually provide for a healthy lifestyle that is reflected in how you feel and interact with others in the workplace.

Weight control is an area of great concern to many people and one that most people struggle with as they age. Research shows that our bodies need less food as we age since metabolism slows with the aging process. This is why a regular exercise program is very important. If you choose to lose weight, you should consider a balanced approach that includes advice from your physician. There are many formal programs for weight loss and maintenance that can provide the formal structure you may need. Maintaining a healthy body weight can contribute to your professional image in the workplace. A healthy weight is important because of the resulting health benefits and how these benefits affect well-being and self-confidence rather than just appearance.

Health Care Assistance

It is important for your health to have regular visits with your physician, dentist, and optometrist. If you are a healthy person with no apparent health problems, you should plan to see your physician at least once a year for a checkup. Usually, this will include some tests and a physical examination. This annual visit is important since it can help identify problems while they are still in the early stages. You should plan to see your dentist at least twice a year for a cleaning and checkup of your teeth. This visit is also important in the maintenance of good oral hygiene and the prevention of serious problems. You should schedule visits every two to three years with an optometrist to check your eyesight. Of course, if you are experiencing any sight problems, you should see an optometrist immediately. You should view your physician, dentist, and optometrist as partners in the maintenance of good health and in helping you maintain a healthy professional image.

RECAP OF KEY CONCEPTS

- A professional image begins with solid grooming, exercise, health, and nutrition habits.

- Professional image is a total package of how you appear and behave.

- It is important to assess your individual body attributes to make wise clothing selections and take care of yourself.

- A professional projects a well-groomed image by having clean and neat hair, teeth, nails, and makeup.

- Hairstyles should be attractive and easy to maintain as well as appropriate for your facial shape. Regular maintenance of your hairstyle should include cutting and coloring, if used.

- Nails should always be neat and clean. If nail polish is used, it should be maintained to avoid projecting a poor image.

- Makeup enhances the overall facial appearance and should be natural in tone and application.

- Regular exercise can reduce stress and help control body weight. Regular exercise can help the professional feel and perform better in the business environment. Good health habits contribute to a professional's overall feeling of wellness.

- A proper diet has a direct relationship to how you feel. You should seek to consume a well-balanced diet that provides enough vitamins and minerals for a healthy body.

- Regular visits to your physician, dentist, and optometrist are an important part of your health routine.

3
Professional Dress

AT THE CORE
This topic examines:

➤ **PROFESSIONAL DRESS DEFINED**
➤ **THE SIGNIFICANCE OF PROFESSIONAL DRESS**
➤ **CRITERIA FOR CLOTHING SELECTION**
➤ **PROFESSIONAL DRESS FOR WOMEN**
➤ **ACCESSORIES FOR WOMEN**
➤ **PROFESSIONAL DRESS FOR MEN**
➤ **ACCESSORIES FOR MEN**
➤ **CASUAL BUSINESS DRESS**
➤ **SPECIAL-OCCASION BUSINESS ATTIRE**

hen you enter the workplace each day, you bring knowledge and expertise about your profession that you acquire through a variety of experiences. These experiences include your educational background, your job experience, and the observation of others. You present your expertise through your job performance, and you present yourself through clothing and appearance. Your clothing and appearance are the wrapping, if you will, in which you choose to place yourself for presentation in the world of work. In her book *Professional Presence*, Susan Bixler maintains, "Although time marches on and trends and influences directly affect our choices in business clothing, three things haven't changed.

1. If you want the job, you have to look the part.
2. If you want the promotion, you have to look promotable.
3. If you want respect, you have to dress as well as or better than your industry standards.[1]"

Your professional packaging communicates many things about you. It reflects commitment to your job, respect for company policies, and judgment in the selection of appropriate clothing for your profession. Your clothing and appearance represent an opportunity to market yourself in a positive way to your peers, your supervisors, and the customers or clients with whom you interact on a daily basis.

> **TIP**   Your clothing is the professional packaging in the business environment.

Your professional dress makes an impression on others through nonverbal communication. Professional dress can affect you positively or negatively throughout your career; therefore, it is important to know how to dress appropriately in the business world. As standards have shifted in some professions, you need to understand and interpret the "rules of dress" as they relate to your professional image. These guidelines will assist you in developing a professional wardrobe:

©PhotoDisc, Inc.

- Know the difference between fashion, fad, and classic styles.
- Wear classic styles in the business environment.
- Strive for quality in clothing purchases.
- Plan your wardrobe.
- Know the best styles and colors for your body type.
- Coordinate your wardrobe items for maximum wear.
- Select appropriate and well-coordinated accessories, such as shoes, belts, ties, scarves, stockings, and socks.

Professional Dress Defined

Professional dress can be defined as dressing in such a manner as to enhance your authority, promote your respect, aid in your promotion, and promote your advancement in the workplace. Professional dress involves making choices about how you will present yourself through your clothing and appearance in the work environment. You have a role that you are expected to perform in your profession, and your appearance and dress are elements of that role. As you look at the definition of professional dress, pay close attention to some of the key phrases. These include the following:

- Enhance your authority. It is important to communicate your authority and position through your dress.
- Promote your respect. Everyone wants to be respected in the work environment, and appropriate clothing contributes to your respectability.
- Aid in your promotion. Most people want to achieve positions of greater responsibility with increased earning capacity in their career. Professional dress can contribute significantly to your image.
- Promote your advancement. This is an important aspect of professional dress. Your dress should not inhibit your career advancement.

> **TIP** Authority, respect, promotion, and advancement are all affected by your professional dress.

Professional dressing is a personal topic and may be an area you find difficult and challenging to manage in your pursuit of developing a professional image. It may be helpful to identify the characteristics of professional dress. These can help guide you in your selection of clothing. Professional dress is:

- consistent with other professionals in your organization.
- comfortable and fits appropriately.
- not offensive to others and does not draw negative attention.
- well-maintained and clean.
- appropriate for the occasion.
- coordinated to create an appropriate look.

Many sources are available for assistance, such as the Internet, books, magazines, and company policies; however, you should also observe the dress of successful and respected people in your profession and in your organization. The environment in which you work is known as the corporate culture. It is the essence of how your company works and the internal practices unique to your organization. You must be observant to determine the unwritten rules of your corporate culture. It is quite common for unwritten rules to apply to dress and appearance. You should dress for where you want to go in your career, not where you are today.

> **TIP** Dress for the position of your future—not the position you have today.

The Significance of Professional Dress

As mentioned earlier, professional dress is your packaging. The people with whom you interact each day see this packaging and make judgments about you. You may think this is somewhat unfair, but people make judgments based on what they see. Sometimes they have the opportunity to change their opinion after learning more about someone or something, but initially, it is someone's or something's appearance that usually determines first impressions. In the business environment, there may not be an opportunity to change the first impression of a customer or potential employer. Some experts say that a first impression is made within seven seconds of the initial meeting.

When you are interacting with customers, they expect professional and appropriate dress from you. Potential employers expect you to show respect for their company and your possible role in that company by dressing appropriately for job interviews. As you progress through your career, employers are evaluating your professional image as they consider you for promotions and advanced positions of responsibility in the workplace. Most of these evaluations occur on a subconscious level, but nonetheless, they occur. A person's success in the business world is usually a combination of several factors. These include:

- Job knowledge.
- Human relations.
- Dress and appearance.

It is important to recognize the significance of dress and appearance as a factor in your career advancement. You should consider your professional dress as a distinguishing characteristic affecting your career advancement that you can control. If you view your professional appearance as a significant ingredient to success, you will be recognized as respecting this element of your professional image. Appearance also affects your self-esteem. When you feel good about the way you look and about your image, you project a positive attitude. This is also true about others' perceptions of you as they relate to your professional dress. You have the opportunity to communicate positively to others through your professional dress, and this is an opportunity you should seize.

> **TIP** You communicate a sense of confidence when you are dressed appropriately.

Criteria for Clothing Selection

Everyone does not and should not dress the same way in the business environment. It is important to recognize distinctive criteria for determining how you should dress in your professional environment. Each of these criteria should be considered when you select clothing for your professional image development. Some of these criteria include the following:

- Type of profession.
- Company policies on dress and appearance.
- Customer and client expectations.
- Geographic location.
- Clothing care and maintenance.
- Appropriate styles, colors, and fabrics.
- Type and frequency of events.
- Budget and purchasing.

Type of Profession. You must know what clothing is appropriate for your profession. For example, a management trainee with a financial institution would dress more formally than a salesperson with an organization selling outdoor furniture and calling on customers in a less formal environment. There are usually accepted rules of professional dress that are unique to each profession, and these should be identified, observed, and practiced. However, there are times when everyone in an organization must recognize that his or her appearance needs to be more formal. This is where your observation of others is important. Do not hesitate to make inquiries about dress if you are unsure about the appropriate attire.

> **TIP** Always ask about the expected or appropriate dress if you are unsure.

Company Policies on Dress and Appearance. Depending on the size and nature of the organization, you may find written policies on professional dress and appearance. You may even find that your company has unwritten practices about dress and appearance. Regardless of whether the policies and/or practices are in writing, you need to identify them. Remember, you want to dress for the position of your future and not necessarily where you are today. You should inquire about written policies and review these to assist you in following the established standard. Always take time to observe others in your organization who are successful and respected in their positions to determine how they present themselves in the work environment.

> **TIP** Take time to observe successful people in your organization and profession to determine how they dress and behave.

Customer and Client Expectations. As an employee of an organization, you represent the organization and may frequently communicate with customers and clients. Therefore, you must determine the appropriate professional dress for interaction with customers and clients. Customers have certain expectations about the professional role of representatives of a company. For instance, a customer who enters a financial institution for a loan usually does not expect to find the loan officer in casual dress because the environment for most financial institutions is more formal than this. On the

©PhotoDisc, Inc.

other hand, if you are a man selling pools and spas, your customers probably do not expect you to call on them in a dark suit, white shirt, and tie.

> **TIP**   Customers have expectations about the professional image of businesspeople.

If you know you will be representing your organization to a conservative customer or client in a more formal business setting, you should dress more conservatively and formal. You must think about your appearance and plan for your personal presentation. Jill Bremer, AICI, in her article, "Making Business Casual Work For You," suggests that you "remember always to consider your industry, your position, and your activities for the day. If you will have any customer contact, think hard about the messages you want to convey and how you can make your client feel at ease. Match their level of dress and the lines of communication will open for you."[2]

Geographic Location.   Different parts of the country require different types of clothing. In the southern part of the country, a linen suit is popular business attire for the female professional during the summer months. In the northeastern part of the country, a linen suit may not be as popular due to the difference in climate. Men who do not work in the warmer sections of the country usually purchase suits with a higher wool content and probably have fewer light-colored blazers than men in warmer climates. Regardless of the climate, certain standards of professional dress should be observed. Even if the temperature is high, you must avoid dressing overly casual so you represent your organization in a professional manner. Refrain from wearing clothing that is too sheer or thin and scanty. Although sleeveless shirts may be comfortable and cool, they are not professional in most business environments. You should pay attention to fabric weight and content so you can manage climate conditions through the selection of appropriate fabrics for your region of the country. Regional differences do exist regarding appropriate professional dress. Do your homework, and determine what is best for your particular area.

Clothing Care and Maintenance. All clothing requires care and maintenance to maintain its look of professionalism for the work environment. You should be aware of the care required of clothing as you select your professional wardrobe. Some fabrics, such as silk, require special cleaning and may be costly to maintain. As you select clothes for your professional wardrobe, always consider the cost of maintaining the fabrics and the availability of this care. A garment can quickly become expensive to own if its care is costly and frequent. Another factor to consider in the care and maintenance of clothing is your time. Try to select a variety of clothes that do not demand too much of your time or money.

Appropriate Styles, Colors, and Fabrics. As you select clothing for your professional wardrobe, you must select styles, colors, and fabrics appropriate for your individual body type. You should assess your body shape, skin tone, and features so you can determine whether a garment or an outfit is appropriate for you. Your goal is to select clothing that best compliments your individual body shape by minimizing areas of concern and enhancing positive features. This applies to everyone. Famous people who are known for their attractive appearance often are very clear on what they can and cannot wear. They know what looks good on their particular body type.

> **TIP**   Color is an important aspect of clothing selection and should compliment your skin tone and be appropriate for the business environment.

Everyone has a unique body shape, and some have what may appear to be an ideal body shape. However, this is rarely the case. Most people in the work environment are average people with average body shapes, and most of them have something they need to enhance and something they need to downplay. The average person is not a model for a men's or women's fashion magazine. As you mature in your professional image development, try to determine the best styles, colors, and shapes for you. Your goal should be to find clothing that makes you look attractive and professional but is still comfortable as well as appropriate. Selecting clothing with proper fit will be presented in more detail later in this module.

Color is another important aspect of clothing selection. The primary color of your suit should be one of the conservative, basic colors. For the male professional, charcoal gray is a classic color. The female professional should select basic primary colors in her suits for maximum wear from her wardrobe. If you know of a color that is not especially flattering to you, avoid this color—regardless of its popularity.

Types and Frequency of Events. As you build your professional wardrobe, you must determine what types of events you are required to attend and the frequency of these events. The types of events determine what type of clothing to purchase, and the frequency of the events determine the number and variety of items required in your wardrobe. If you regularly make presentations to top-level executives, you need to have more formal business attire, that is, suits for men and business suits and dresses for women. The number of events you must attend determines how many different outfits are required, which is important in planning your clothing purchases.

Budget and Purchasing. Clothing management should be like any other aspect of your career. You should plan for purchases and consider this part of your budget. Your professional wardrobe is an investment in your career; planning and managing it is important. Clothing can be expensive; therefore, you must develop sound purchasing techniques for maximizing your clothing budget. You should view each purchase as a contribution to your overall professional wardrobe and determine how it will benefit your wardrobe. Make sure you spend the majority of your clothing budget on clothing that will "earn" rewards in your professional image development.

> **TIP** Spend the majority of your clothing dollars on wardrobe items that will earn you money and rewards in your professional image.

Professional Dress for Women

The female business person has a wide variety of clothing styles, colors, and fabrics from which to choose when selecting a professional wardrobe. Because of this variety, she may have difficulty determining what is appropriate in the business environment. The same general rules and guidelines for professional dress apply to both men and women. Remember, you are trying to "enhance your authority, promote your respect, aid in your promotion, and promote your advancement."

For a professional woman in a formal business environment, the skirted suit or pantsuit with a single-breasted two-to three-button jacket is the most common basic attire. This attire communicates a message of business and formality to everyone with whom the female professional comes in contact. The suit is the foundation for the professional woman's wardrobe and should represent her biggest monetary investment.

©PhotoDisc, Inc.

Certain variations of this basic attire include dresses with jackets, other skirts or pants to expand the wardrobe, and appropriate accessories.

A jacket is a powerful clothing item for both men and women. While wearing a jacket, you are communicating a more authoritative image; you are communicating a more formal and stronger business message. Women should be mindful of this as they consider their presentation methods and establish their credibility in the business world through professional image.

Most women have several suits and dresses as their basic wardrobe items. The length of a skirt is determined by a woman's height and overall build. A long skirt is usually more flattering and more accommodating for the demands of a business day. However, if you are a petite woman, a skirt that is too long may seem to cover your entire body. Short skirts are not appropriate in the workplace. Bixler recommends that the length of the skirt be "most flattering to both your leg and your profession."[3] You should pay close attention to your selection of an appropriate skirt length. You can determine this by trying on several lengths and keeping in mind what you must do in your job each day. If your skirt is so short that you are constantly trying to keep it pulled down, then it is definitely too short.

Bixler also recommends the business dress as an alternative to the suit. She states, "Although they do not have the same amount of power or authority that a suit does, they are more comfortable and often more feminine."[4] A woman's wardrobe should also contain several pairs of classic slacks and skirts in basic colors such as black, navy, and taupe or khaki. The wardrobe should be further extended with coordinating jackets and shirts that are interchangeable with slacks and skirts to create numerous outfits. A well-coordinated wardrobe should be interchangeable and versatile so a minimum amount of time is spent on finding pieces that work well together. As you are building your wardrobe, be mindful that you should begin with basic colors and avoid colors that are too stark or outrageous.

Accessories for Women

Accessories are a great wardrobe extender and should be considered as a basic component of the wardrobe that requires planning and coordination. For the female, accessories include jewelry, scarves, handbags, hosiery, and shoes.

Jewelry. Jewelry should be simple and not attract too much attention. You should avoid jewelry that creates noise, as this can be distracting in the business environment. For example, a charm bracelet that jingles whenever you move your arm is not appropriate for the business world. You should also avoid overuse of jewelry. For instance, do not wear a ring on every finger or more than one bracelet. You also want to select jewelry that is appropriate in size for your body. For instance, a larger woman would want to wear larger earrings or a wider bracelet. A smaller woman with a short haircut would want to wear smaller jewelry.

Most professional women wear simple earrings, a necklace or lapel pin, a watch, and one or two rings to complete their jewelry. Jewelry can be gold or silver but should coordi-

©PhotoDisc, Inc.

nate with your wardrobe. If you wear sterling silver, you need to keep it polished to maintain its luster. Costume jewelry tends to lose its finish after a period of wear and will need to be replaced. It may be preferable to own a few pieces of good jewelry rather than many pieces of costume jewelry. Also, pearls provide a classic look to most business attire.

TIP Avoid wearing too much jewelry or jewelry that makes noise.

Scarves. A scarf can add a distinctive look to your professional wardrobe. You should first learn how to tie a scarf so it stays in place and looks attractive. Bixler suggests that the best scarf is "one that stays in place when tied and actually contributes to the pulling together of an outfit. It should not clutter or overwhelm. The most useful shape is oblong because it can be wrapped in many different ways, including the ascot."[5] When selecting a scarf, you can coordinate colors or use contrasting colors to enhance the look of your outfit. A scarf should be worn to create a different look or to finish the look of the neckline of your blouse or jacket. You should experiment with scarves and learn how to tie them for the enhancements they can provide your wardrobe.

Handbags. Care should be given to the selection of an appropriate handbag for your professional image. Your handbag should not be too large as to overwhelm your professional look. Your handbag should be moderate in size and should not be overfilled. An overstuffed handbag with items falling out does not contribute to a professional image. You should select a handbag with enough structure to maintain its shape and hold

©PhotoDisc, Inc.

the contents in place. Handbags with a substantial lining are also preferred over handbags without a lining. The professional uses her handbag to store necessary items and does not put too much in the bag. If you carry only the items you need, you will be able to find them easily and will avoid that overfilled look. Your handbag should coordinate closely with your shoes. A leather handbag in a dark color will serve you well during the winter and fall seasons. For the summer, a lighter-colored leather or tightly woven fabric is appropriate.

Hosiery. Hosiery should be selected to compliment the business wardrobe. You should select neutral tones that blend with the hemline. Select darker colors and heavier weights for the winter and lighter weights for the summer.[6] Never wear stockings that are darker than your shoes, which creates a negative visual effect. Avoid wearing trouser socks or knee-high stockings with a dress or skirt. Trouser socks or knee-highs are made to wear with slacks, not with skirts or dresses. You should always wear stockings with a dress or suit. It is not acceptable, regardless of the temperature, to go without stockings in a business setting. If you are wearing slacks, you should select a coordinating trouser sock. The stockings should be long enough to provide adequate coverage when your legs are crossed and not expose your legs.

Shoes. You should select quality, comfortable shoes for your business wardrobe. Shoes are considered a major accessory and should finish off an outfit. You should select a quality leather shoe with a moderate-height heel. Shoes should generally be close to the color of your skirt or slacks. You want to avoid too much contrast between the color of your dress, skirt, or slacks and your shoes. Spillane and Sherlock suggest quality leather, neutral colors, coordinated color with the hemline, and midheel or pumps. They also suggest avoiding seasonal fashion colors with limited life, heels that prevent you from walking normally, and white in any style.[7]

Professional Dress for Men

For the male professional, the basic suit has been an established uniform of the business world for years. The dark suit in an all-wool tropical weight is considered the foundation of the male wardrobe. This provides the wearer with a wide variety of options for coordination.[8] The male professional has a variety of fabric weights and content from which to choose. The majority of business suits are constructed of a combination of fabrics such as wool, cotton, and/or polyester. The wool content gives weight to the construction and ensures wearability for years. Even suits that are traditionally worn in the summer months usually contain some wool fabric.

The most formal business attire is a dark suit with a white shirt and tie. Most male professionals have at least two or three basic business suits as the foundation for their wardrobe—even more if they must wear them everyday. The basic wardrobe for the male professional can be extended with coordinating jackets and slacks. Suggestions for these include a navy blue blazer; tweed sports coat; coordinating slacks in navy, khaki, or black; and a variety of shirts. Some experts consider the navy blazer an essential element of the male professional's wardrobe.[9] You need to consider the weight and content of the fabrics when coordinating different wardrobe pieces. For instance, you would never wear a linen jacket with wool pants. The trousers that accompany a suit may be cuffed or straight. Bixler suggests that shorter, heavier men avoid cuffs. Most pleated trousers are cuffed, and the hem should fall with a slight break in the front at the shoe level.[10] The design of the pattern of the fabric for the suit can vary from a pinstripe to a tweed to a herringbone effect. The pinstripe is a traditional classic pattern that is always in good taste and appropriate for the business environment. You should be careful when choosing a tweed pattern and select colors that coordinate with your solid trousers and shirts. Meehan suggests that the "keys to matching colors are to work around your base color and to understand what works best with that particular color. The base color is the dominant color in the suit or sports coat.[11]

Shirts. The male professional's wardrobe should contain several white shirts of high-quality cotton and several coordinating solid-colored dress shirts to wear with a suit and/or other jackets. The collection of shirts should be completed with several striped shirts (preferably a blue stripe) to coordinate with a dark suit. Attention to the selection of a quality shirt is very important in the attainment of a finished and polished look. Shirts should be well-constructed and have quality detail at the collar, neck, and cuffs. When selecting a shirt, you should have ample room to button the shirt comfortably at the neck and have enough sleeve length to allow you to button the cuffs comfortably with approximately one-half to three-quarters of an inch extending beyond the suit sleeve.

Accessories for Men

©PhotoDisc, Inc.

The male professional has a variety of accessory items from which to choose. These include ties, belts, shoes, socks, and hats. Attention to the coordination of these items will result in a more effective overall appearance. Remember that you must consider the total picture when putting a wardrobe together.

Ties. Ties are considered a basic accessory garment for the male professional and are a great way to give the wardrobe variety. However, care should be given to the selection of appropriate ties. Ties should compliment the suit; if a striped shirt is worn with a suit, the tie should be a solid or appropriately coordinated design. Meehan suggests that the male professional maintain an inventory of six to ten red or burgundy ties. These colors go well with the dark classic business suit. He further recommends that tie patterns should be varied between stripes, paisleys, foulards, and modern. Yellow is also suggested for gray or navy suits. Navy ties go well with light gray or camel-colored sports coats. Green ties coordinate nicely with tan and navy. The tie should fall approximately at the center or bottom of the belt at the waist.[12]

Belts, Shoes, and Socks. The selection of a belt, shoes, and socks requires attention to ensure that the wardrobe is well-coordinated. The leather belt is considered another basic accessory item in the professional male's wardrobe. Attention should be given to selecting a quality leather belt in a dark finish, such as dark brown or black. Your belt should match your shoes.[13] Most wardrobes require at least two leather belts—one in a dark color, such as black, and a second in a lighter shade of brown. Shoes should coordinate with the belt, and socks should closely match the color of the slacks. Socks should not attract attention. Shoes of quality leather that are both comfortable and functional should be selected.

Hats. Hats are another accessory for the professional male's wardrobe. Usually hats are worn in the colder climates of the country and coordinate with the coat. A hat should always be removed after entering a building.

Casual Business Dress

The concept of business casual dressing has developed rapidly in the business world in the last decade. However, probably no other concept regarding professional dress has caused as much confusion and misinterpretation than business casual. Rather than helping many people in the business world, it sometimes leads to confusion about what to wear and what is expected. Some people think they need to purchase another wardrobe for the Friday practice of "casual day." Still others interpret this to mean "anything goes." For the employer, it sometimes presents serious situations when employees select inappropriate clothing for the workplace, resulting in embarrassment to both the employer and the customers. For this reason, many policies have been written in the corporate world that address this aspect of professional dress. Sometimes these policies emphasize what people cannot wear rather than what they can wear.

©Digital Vision

In addition, some companies have now gone to a company uniform for casual day that may be distributed or purchased for this style of dress. Lands' End, a clothing manufacturer and catalog retailer, has developed a line of clothing especially for corporate sales. The *Spring 2002 Catalog* offers suggestions of apparel for "trade shows, corporate casual, recruitment, sales, and client meetings."[14] In any event, recognize that business is conducted every day the organization is open to the public; therefore, the appropriateness of dress is important every day as well.

Regardless of what day is showing on the calendar, you must remember what your role is for that day and who you will be working and interacting with on behalf of your organization. If you work for an organization that has a business casual day, you should follow the basic principle of maintaining a professional appearance. For most women, this means wearing a skirt or slacks with a sweater or casual jacket. For men, this may mean wearing slacks and a shirt without a tie. Both men and women should consider the following guidelines on clothing selection for casual dress days. Clothes should be:

- Clean and well-maintained with no stains or tears.
- Structured and not excessively loose-fitting.
- Cover the body.
- An appropriate color and style for the business environment.
- Appropriate for meeting the public and representing the company in a positive manner.

In addition to clothing being appropriate for business casual days, your personal appearance should also be appropriate. You should be well-groomed, and your hair, nails, and accessories should positively represent the company.

Special-Occasion Business Attire

Most business professionals must attend special events related to their job. Some of these occasions include conferences or conventions, presentations, company parties or social events, and funerals and weddings. If you are attending any of these events as a representative of your company, you should be mindful of your appearance and how this will be associated with your company. For instance, you may be attending a conference where the style of dress is somewhat casual; however, you are still a representative of your organization. This is a setting where you may be networking with other professionals and want to make a positive impression on others.

For presentations, you should recognize that people give a great deal of attention to what you are wearing and how you appear as well as to what you are saying. You want to select clothing that does not detract from your message to the audience. Do not let your clothes speak negatively for you. The best rule to follow is to choose conservative and classic clothing. For social events, your clothing certainly depends on the type of event. If you are attending a company picnic or golf outing, appropriate-length shorts and a casual shirt are in order. For a more formal company party or social event (such as a cocktail party), you would select formal clothing that is both conservative and appropriate. When attending these types of events, you might inquire about expected attire. Always ask if you do not know what to wear.

Most professionals maintain a few basic items in their wardrobe for these events. For the male business person, it is usually the dark suit or tuxedo, if indicated. For the female, it is the conservative, solid-colored dress. The simple black dress has become a classic for the female professional. Accented with simple pearls or jewelry, this is a classic look that communicates a positive professional image. If you must attend a great number of special events, you will need to expand these items in your wardrobe.

RECAP OF KEY CONCEPTS

- You present your professional image through your performance and your appearance.
- Quality classic styles are appropriate in the business world for both men and women.
- Professional dress is dressing to enhance your authority, promote your respect, aid in your promotion, and promote your advancement in the business world.
- Professional dress can significantly affect your career, as does your job knowledge and your human relations skills.
- Criteria for clothing selection include the type of profession; company policies; customer expectations; geographic location; clothing care; styles, colors and fabrics; types of events; and budget resources.
- The basic dress for a female professional is a skirted suit or pantsuit.
- The basic dress for a male professional is a business suit in a dark color.
- Accessories for women include jewelry, scarves, handbags, hosiery, and shoes. All of these items should be well-coordinated and compliment the basic outfit.
- Accessories for men include ties, belts, shoes, socks, and hats. These should be well-coordinated and compliment the basic outfit.
- Casual dress should be professional in its overall appearance. To ensure appropriateness, casual dress should be clean and structured, cover the body, be an appropriate color and style, and be appropriate for meeting the public.
- A professional's wardrobe should include items for special occasions such as cocktail parties, receptions, conferences, weddings, and funerals.

4
Wardrobe Management

An important aspect of professional dress is the development and maintenance of an appropriate and functional wardrobe. You want to develop a wardrobe that contains all the essentials you need to present yourself daily in a professional manner. You also want a wardrobe that is appropriate for your work style, fits properly, requires minimum maintenance, and is within your budget. It takes time and planning to accomplish these objectives for your wardrobe, but once the basics are established, you will find the ongoing care of your wardrobe not to be excessively time-consuming. Remember that managing your wardrobe is an important aspect of managing your professional career and, therefore, requires attention.

Individual Style

In the previous topic, you were presented with the basics of a professional wardrobe and what it should contain. In this topic, you will personalize the professional wardrobe to meet your individual needs. The first step in managing your wardrobe is determining what is appropriate for you within the basic guidelines of developing a professional image as it relates to clothing. You must assess several factors prior to making purchases to ensure maximum benefits. These factors include size and body type, color, and style. Each of these factors is unique for every individual and must be determined through careful assessment.

Size and Body Type. Every person has his or her own unique size and body shape. It may seem that there is an ideal male or female body shape, but this really is not the case. Everyone has something he or she wants to accent and something he or she chooses to de-emphasize. If you are a woman, you should determine whether you are petite, average, or tall in height. You then need to determine your body type. Mary Spillane and Christine Sherlock have identified seven main body types for women with recommendations for what looks best. These include:

1. Inverted triangle—sharp, crisp styles; does not accentuate shoulders; accents the body with simple designs and color rather than patterns
2. Straight—looks good in tightly woven fabrics; sharply structured or unstructured lines; avoid gathers at the waist, but pleats look good
3. Softened straight—modified version of straight; can emphasize the waist; pleats and gathers used in moderation; keep fabrics, designs, and cuts more defined; fitted-cut jackets
4. Angular pear—key accessory is shoulder pads; want to balance shoulders with hips; peaked or pointed lapels on jackets are good; layering works on the top portion of the body; waist should fit closely with plenty of room for hips
5. Curved pear—need to balance figure with shoulder pads; use soft pleats or gathers at waist, but avoid these completely around the waist; boat necklines are good; avoid slim-fitting tops; choose soft fabrics
6. Hourglass—be careful with fabric and design; cut of clothes should be soft and easy; avoid set-in sleeves; lapels should be rounded; waist should be accentuated; avoid loose and baggy tops if full-busted

7. Round—keep look unstructured; avoid attention to the waistline; longer jackets are preferred; shoulder pads can be a good accessory; avoid too much draping to add volume[1]

Each of these body types has advantages and disadvantages. You should be familiar with your body type so you can select clothing that is flattering to you and that projects the best professional image.

If you are a man, you want to be familiar with your body build so you can select clothes with the correct lengths and lines to fit your body. As a man, you may have an average, portly, or long build. This is important in the selection of suits. Suits are sized and constructed according to these different body types. Meehan recommends that men consider "height, weight, and overall build when selecting a style of suit." He further recommends the "three-button coat for broad-chested men with a fuller torso because of the lapels and straighter cut of the coat. The two-button coat usually has longer lapels with front darts and generally fits men who are slender and require some tapering in the body of the coat."[2] Clothing styles are made for different body shapes, and professionals who are familiar with their body style and select clothing accordingly will look more professional in their overall appearance.

Color. Color is also a factor you should consider in clothing selection. Different colors look best on different people. You should take the time to determine what colors look best with your skin tone and select colors that compliment your appearance. Color can also affect the overall appearance of size and shape according to the hue and location. For instance, the warm colors of yellow, orange, and gold have a tendency to enlarge an object; whereas the cool colors of blue, green, and blue reds have a tendency to maintain an object's size. Black is well-known for its slimming effect on most people.

Where the color is located is also important to body shape. Spillane and Sherlock introduce several "color tricks" for women. These include drawing attention to the face with your best colors, avoiding light colors on the bottom portion as they tend to enlarge, and avoiding black if it is not pleasing to your complexion. They also recommend that petite women dress in one color to avoid the effect of breaking the body into pieces. They recommend that petite women coordinate the color of their hosiery with the color of their skirt and shoes to get a longer look. Taller women can wear more blocks of color but should be careful of this in the business environment as it can create an unprofessional look.[3] In general, if you want to minimize the upper body, you should wear a lighter color near the face with a darker color on the bottom portion of the body. When desiring an overall smaller effect, you should select clothes of the same material and color for both the top and bottom.

> **TIP**   The use of color can be a powerful tool in your professional dress wardrobe.

Lines. Another factor in clothing style is that of the lines created by clothes. Every point where you see a "line" creates volume. Lines are created with color or seams or where clothes fall on the body. For instance, if you have wide hips and you wear a jacket that ends at the widest point, you have created a "line" and emphasized this location on your body. However, if you wear a longer jacket over the hips or above the widest point, you do not bring as much emphasis to this location. Women who have a large bust do not want extra darts or sleeves that end in the bust area. The same goes for the length of a skirt. Avoid lengths that end where your legs are the largest.

> **TIP**   A line can be created with a seam, the end of a garment, or a color. Attention is always drawn to a line; therefore, use lines wisely.

The length of pants for a man can create the same effect. It is important that pants not be too long on a shorter man, as this creates a shorter image. Cuffed pants are usually more appropriate for taller men. The double-breasted jacket can create too much volume in the center area of a broader man and may not be the best selection.

Wardrobe Assessment and Planning

An important aspect of developing and maintaining a professional wardrobe is assessing your needs and determining your initial priorities. Consideration should be given to all of the elements mentioned in the previous topic. Consider the following: type of profession, company policies, job expectations, and budget. Begin by reviewing the type of profession you are entering or working in. Ask yourself questions about the types of professional dress that are required to be successful in your profession. Make sure you consider the individual climate of your organization and the policies and expectations regarding dress, and plan for expenditures that will allow you to stay within your budget. The business suit has been identified as the most appropriate attire for both men and women in the business environment. The following items are recommended for the basic wardrobe of a woman:

- One to two business suits
- Two solid jackets
- Three pairs of slacks in solid colors to coordinate with jackets
- Four to five blouses or shirts
- Two business dresses in a simple, tailored style
- One formal-occasion dress or suit
- One casual sweater or jacket
- One all-weather coat or raincoat in year-round fabric
- Two pairs of dress shoes
- One pair of flat casual shoes
- Two leather belts
- One leather purse
- One briefcase

©PhotoDisc, Inc.

> **TIP** It takes time to build your professional wardrobe, so plan and purchase wisely.

The following items are recommended for the basic wardrobe of a man:

- One to two dark suits
- One sports coat or solid-colored blazer
- Three pairs of solid-colored slacks to coordinate with the sports coat or blazer
- Five solid-colored dress shirts
- Two striped shirts or casual shirts

- Five or six business ties
- Two pairs of dress shoes
- One all-weather coat or raincoat in a year-round fabric
- Two leather belts
- One leather briefcase

©PhotoDisc, Inc.

You should inventory what you have in your closet that meets your minimum requirements for professional dress, then make a list of your purchasing needs in priority order. With this inventory and your priorities established, you are ready to begin purchasing appropriate clothing for your professional wardrobe.

Making Clothing Purchases

Making wise clothing purchases involves several ingredients to be successful. Several helpful techniques for effective shopping include the following:

- *Make a list of necessary items.* The first step presented in the previous section was to identify needs on a priority basis. You should keep a working list of necessary items, as this will help you keep your wardrobe needs in mind as you shop. This will also allow you to take advantage of shopping opportunities such as regular sales and clearance promotions. If you know you need an item of clothing, finding it on sale is a financial opportunity not to be missed.
- *Allow adequate time to shop.* You must also allow yourself enough time to be able to evaluate the different clothing items available in the retail market. Most people do not consider shopping for their professional wardrobe a serious endeavor, but they should. You should allocate adequate time for this activity so you can evaluate and consider how the clothing looks on you, how it coordinates with other pieces in your wardrobe, and how it fits the professional requirements of your career. Rarely is this accomplished in a rushed and hurried manner. As you develop your techniques of purchasing, shopping may take less time, but it will always require a focused effort. You should select a time of day when you are able to concentrate on the selection of your clothing in an environment that is

conducive to this activity. For instance, you may find that early morning, when the stores are less crowded, is better for you than after work, when you are tired and the stores are more crowded. If you choose to take someone with you, make sure that person knows what you are looking for and will provide appropriate feedback on how an item looks or its value to your career wardrobe.

> **TIP** It takes quality time to select appropriate clothing for your professional image.

- *Become familiar with the clothing stores in your area.* You should know the retail market in your area or in an area you may travel to for purchases. Certain stores specialize in clothing that is more appropriate for the business environment, and it is especially helpful to know which ones cater to the business professional. It is also important to know which stores allow complimentary alterations, as these may be necessary for proper fit. Some stores also have special sales or promotions at the same time of year, which allow you to make purchases at a savings. In addition, some stores have special complimentary shopping consultants who can help advise you about purchases. All of these features are available at larger stores and are worth investigating.

- *Wear the proper clothing for shopping.* When you are purchasing clothing for the business environment, you should wear the undergarments and shoes that you will be wearing with these clothes. Even if you must carry along your dress shoes, it is worth the effort since you will be able to see how the dress or suit you have tried on looks with your existing shoes. This is important for both men and women. It is difficult to envision your tailored suit with tennis shoes.

- *Examine the quality of the garments you are considering.* It is important to invest your wardrobe dollars in well-constructed garments that will wear well and will last for a long period of time. Remember that paying a high price for a product does not ensure quality; nor does paying a low price mean poor quality. There are bargains in apparel selection that can help you stretch your dollars, but you should remember that regardless of price, if the garment is poorly constructed and does not fit into your wardrobe, it is not a bargain.

To ensure that you are purchasing quality clothing, make sure that you examine the construction in key areas. Such areas include these:

- Well-attached buttons
- Extra buttons—especially if the buttons are unique
- Well-attached hems
- Buttonholes that do not show the lining of the inside fabric
- Straight seams
- Well-attached belt loops
- Removable shoulder pads in blouses
- Well-attached linings in slacks and jackets to prevent sagging
- Lining fabrics that match the garment
- Sufficient pocket depth on slacks
- Seams that are in the proper location for centering in the back of a jacket; the bustline of a blouse or dress; and the shoulders on all jackets, shirts, and blouses
- Colors that are consistent throughout the garment and that match any accompanying garment
- Matched patterns at seams and hems
- Reinforced areas on jackets such as the collar and lapel

It takes time and effort to ensure that you are getting your money's worth in clothing purchases, but it is well worth it in the end. You will find that your quality purchases last many years. It is not unusual for a well-made men's or woman's suit to last up to five years.

> **TIP**   Quality clothing will be a part of your professional wardrobe for many years, ensuring that you are getting a sound value for your financial expenditures.

- *Purchase classic styles.* Another factor you should consider in your clothing purchases is the ability to separate classic styles, fashion trends, and fads. A classic style should always be your starting point in establishing your wardrobe. You will need these classic items to carry you through your career. It is important to remember that most work environments are not where you want to make a fashion statement. Fashion trends and fads tend to last only one season or less. If a trend or fad is especially attractive to you, you might consider making a purchase for your casual wardrobe. However, you want to refrain from spending excessively on fashion trends or fads because they come and go too quickly to realize any financial value from your money.

Ensuring a Proper Fit

One of the challenges of any wardrobe purchase is to make sure that an item fits properly. Most people have some part of their body that represents a challenge when selecting clothing. However, you can still purchase clothing that is both attractive and functional for your work environment if you learn some basic rules regarding proper fit. Here are some basic principles that apply to all items of clothing.

- Clothing should be attractive and functional.
- Clothing should be reasonably comfortable.
- Clothing should allow you to do your job without worrying about the item during the normal workday.

When ensuring a proper fit, there are several considerations to be made, most of which are unique to the particular item of clothing.

TIP Your clothes must fit properly to be comfortable throughout the workday.

Foundation Garments. Beginning with the foundation, undergarments should provide coverage, be barriers for perspiration, and provide support for the body. Women want to make sure their undergarments do not show through outer fabrics and are, therefore, too revealing. Undergarments should not be so tight that they create an unattractive bulge. If a dress or suit is not lined, a slip is usually needed. In all instances, if a dress or skirt is so sheer that you can see the basic undergarments, a slip or dress liner must be worn to ensure an appropriate professional appearance.

For men, undershirts should always be worn under dress shirts with a suit. This creates a barrier for perspiration and provides a smooth outer finish for the shirt. An undershirt should have an appropriately cut neckline. A round-neck undershirt should not be worn with a shirt that may be unbuttoned during the day. This would require a v-neck undershirt.

Jackets and Blazers. A jacket or blazer should fit smoothly across the upper body. The length of the jacket should generally fall where your fingertips fall when you stand with your hands against your side. For women, a suit jacket may be made to stop at the waist rather than at the hips. If this is the case, the jacket should fall right at the waist, not above or below the waist. The length of the jacket sleeve should provide coverage of the shirt or blouse. No more than half an inch of the shirt or blouse should show from the sleeve. The lapels of the jacket should lie flat and, if notched, should match on both sides. A jacket should fit the body to allow for movement in meetings or presentations.

©Digital Stock

Pants and Skirts. Pants and slacks should fit at the natural waist and allow enough space for the wearer to insert two fingers comfortably. Pants that require a belt should not be so full at the waist as to create folds of fabric underneath the belt. The seat area of the slacks should fit without too much fabric between the main seam and the interior leg seams. Undergarment lines should not show through. The length of pants should fall slightly above the shoe. Women usually wear a moderate heel or a flatter shoe with pants, which should be considered when determining the length of the pants. Both men and women should avoid piling of fabric at the shoe and avoid exposure of the heel area. A professional tailor can ensure proper leveling and length of the finished pants' hem. A skirt length should compliment the style of the jacket and the person's body shape. Petite women usually need to avoid skirts that are too long, as they seem to cover the entire body; whereas longer skirts are an option for taller women. Women should avoid skirts that are too short because they can create a challenge in providing adequate coverage and may not be attractive. The most popular skirt length over a long period of fashion time has been the knee to midcalf length. This ideal and universal length provides an attractive and functional length for most women.

Blouses and Shirts. Blouses and shirts should receive appropriate attention in their selection for proper fit. Buttons should be attached properly, and all areas of construction should be well-sewn to withstand the demands of daily wear. For men, the shirt neck should fit snugly, but not be so tight that it is uncomfortable or creates a wrinkled or stretched look. The arm seams should align with the armpit, with the cuffs of the shirt falling at the wrist and closing comfortably. The length of the shirt should allow approximately one-half inch of the shirt to be exposed from underneath the jacket. Always avoid shirt sleeve lengths that are too short, as this creates a skimpy look. The shirt should fit comfortably across the midsection of the body and close easily without a tight look. The shirt should be long enough to allow at least four to six inches to be tucked into the pants. For women, a blouse should fit across the bust and midriff areas without any tight or pulled look. The arm openings should allow for ease of movement. The sleeve length on a blouse can vary for a woman, but the sleeveless look should be avoided in the professional environment. This is too casual for most business environments. When wearing a long-sleeved blouse, the length should end at the wrist and close comfortably.[4] If the blouse has shoulder pads, these should add definition to the shoulder area and not be too large or obvious. Detachable shoulder pads are preferable over permanently attached ones for ease of maintenance.

TIP A key to proper fit is ensuring that you choose the correct size to allow ample room and to create a pleasing, professional image.

Accessories. Accessories should also "fit" properly. It is important to select accessories that compliment the basic wardrobe. For men, the primary accessory items include belts, ties, socks, and shoes. A belt should fit adequately around the waist and allow closure so that at least 2 inches extends beyond the closure loop. Ties should lie down the center of the shirt and end at or slightly below the belt buckle. Socks should compliment the color of the pants and should be long enough to provide adequate coverage of the ankles and lower leg area, even when the legs are crossed. Shoes should fit comfortably and compliment the color of the pants.

Accessory items for women include scarves, jewelry, stockings, and shoes. Scarves are considered a great wardrobe extender and can create entirely different looks for a wardrobe. Scarves should be of complimentary colors, and the fabric should allow ease of tying and attachment. If you choose to wear a scarf, you should learn how to tie it so you present a pleasing, finished look. Jewelry should be selected with the same criteria; it should compliment the outfit. Generally, women wear lapel pins, earrings, bracelets, and necklaces. Care should be given not to wear too much jewelry and to avoid mixing too many silver and gold pieces. Hosiery color should compliment the skirt or pants and should not create a stark contrast. Hosiery or socks should never be darker than the shoe color. Shoes should be comfortable and functional for the business environment.

> **TIP** The color of your hosiery or socks should not be darker than your shoes.

Wardrobe Budgeting

One of the greatest challenges for any business professional is the selection of quality clothing within a budget. Clothing should be considered an investment in your professional tool inventory; therefore, you should plan to spend a portion of your earnings on the purchase and maintenance of your wardrobe. With careful planning and knowledge about shopping techniques, you can become a wise consumer, stay within your budget, and still maintain a professional wardrobe. The following guidelines will help you in your wardrobe budget management:

- Know what items should receive the most attention in your wardrobe. Generally, a basic suit is the foundation item for men and women. This is the item you will be wearing the most, and this item will receive the most wear and tear; therefore, you should probably spend most of your budget dollars on this basic item.

©PhotoDisc, Inc.

- Become familiar with the stores in your area. You should know which stores carry items for your wardrobe within your budget. Stores also vary on the types of services they make available for their customers. Complimentary alterations and personal shopping services can be invaluable.
- Identify stores that have special purchasing agreements. Many stores offer interest-free accounts if they are paid off within a three- to six-month period. This can be a great purchasing tool for any professional. Inquire at stores in your area about special purchasing agreements, including advance notice of sales and promotions.
- Know which time of year to purchase items. It is important as you build your wardrobe to develop your "needs" list so you can take advantage of special sales at certain times of the year. For instance, the best time to purchase a winter coat is at the end of the winter season. If you purchase a coat at the beginning of the season, you will most likely pay full price. Stores many times have special promotion sales at the beginning of a season to attract customers; this is another buying opportunity to take advantage of.
- Always purchase quality items for your basic wardrobe. Quality clothing in your wardrobe will last for many years. It is not unrealistic to think that you can purchase suits, jackets, blazers, and pants that will last three to five years. Some items can last even longer. Quality construction of a garment, basic styles, and basic colors lend themselves to ensuring longevity. You should always examine the quality of the construction of a garment before purchasing it.
- Consider the cost of care and maintenance of any wardrobe purchase. You must consider the cost of maintaining your wardrobe. Dry-cleaning costs have continued to increase, and any item that requires special and frequent care will end up costing more money regardless of the initial cost. Certain fabrics require specialized cleaning; and these should not be the mainstay of your wardrobe unless you have unlimited funds. Always read the care labels when making a purchase. This will ensure that you know about the care of an item prior to purchasing it.

You can become a wise consumer by taking your time when purchasing clothing, knowing what you need, and making sure that the clothing purchases you make are consistent with your professional requirements.

Wardrobe Care

One important aspect of managing a wardrobe is the care and maintenance of clothes and accessories. Clothes are an investment and should be maintained for longevity and attractiveness over a period of time. With the proper care and maintenance, quality clothing items can last many years, becoming a mainstay of your wardrobe. As mentioned earlier, prior to making a purchase, you should read the care label that is attached to a garment. The fabric and recommended care will determine how each garment is maintained. Clothing with attached shoulder pads, linings, or special attachments require dry cleaning. Some fabrics, such as silk, may even require special dry-cleaning processes. It is important to know this prior to making a purchase. Many other items (such as blouses, undergarments, and more casual clothes) require regular machine washing and pressing. The following guidelines should be followed for routine care of your wardrobe:

- Blouses and shirts should be cleaned after each wearing.
- Suits should be cleaned after five or more wearings.
- All clothes should be cleaned immediately when stained to help remove the stain as quickly as possible.
- All clothes should be pressed for a crisp, unwrinkled look.
- Shoes should be cleaned frequently, and leather should be polished and buffed to maintain its luster.
- Accessories should be checked and cleaned when needed.
- Pants should be pressed with a crease for a professional, finished look.
- All seasonal clothes should be cleaned at the end of the season and stored appropriately for protection.

Clothing care also includes maintenance and repair of items in your wardrobe. Clothes should always be maintained by ensuring that all buttons are replaced, zippers are flat and in good working condition, clasps are firmly attached, hems are in place, and linings are not extended.

> **TIP** Clothes that are well cared for will last much longer than clothes that do not receive proper care and maintenance.

When you wear your clothes for as many as 8 to 12 hours a day, some natural wear and tear does occur. You should be aware of this and examine your clothing frequently to determine if areas are in need of repair. Accessories such as stockings and socks should not have any visible holes or tears. Shoes should be repaired or replaced when torn or worn in places. Many times the worn soles of shoes may be replaced, eliminating the need to purchase a new pair. Leather items such as briefcases, shoes, and handbags should be cleaned with leather cleaner and kept in repair. You should find a reputable person who specializes in clothing alterations and maintenance.

Another important aspect of wardrobe management is how you store your clothing. All items of clothing should have a place in a closet, on a shelf, or in a drawer. Items should be hung up immediately after being worn so they do not wrinkle and their shape is maintained. A good practice is to hang clothes up immediately but not place them between other clothes, letting them "air" for a short period of time. Suits should be hung on sturdy hangers that help maintain the shape of the jacket. Pants should be hung from the waist or folded once over a heavy hanger to reduce creasing. Skirts should be hung on hangers so they can be clipped at the waist to reduce creases. Shirts should be hung so the collars are not pressed down or wrinkled. It is absolutely essential that you have adequate room to store your clothing. A closet that is too full results in clothes that are misplaced, wrinkled and creased. Clothes need enough room to maintain their shape on the hangers. Care should be taken to place clothes appropriately on hangers so they hang correctly. Clothes should be organized in your closet so you can easily assess what is available and get dressed in a reasonable amount of time.

A well-organized closet should have clothes grouped together for ease of access. For instance, all suits should be grouped together with all coordinating shirts and blouses located near the suits for ease of matching. Shoes should be organized so that casual and exercise shoes are separated from dress shoes. Handbags should be stored so they maintain their shape while not in use. Shelves and drawers should be organized so that it is easy to identify the contents. These basic organizational guidelines will help you maintain your wardrobe.

With a basic care routine, organization of your wardrobe, and a professional to help maintain your clothing items, your wardrobe will serve you well for many years. You will be able to realize a value for the money you invested in the wardrobe, and you will project a professional image in the business environment.

RECAP OF KEY CONCEPTS

- ◆ Size, body shape, color, and lines affect your individual clothing style selections.
- ◆ Selection of clothing should be based on type of profession, company policies, job expectations, and budget. The business suit with a skirt or pants is the foundation of the professional woman's wardrobe. The business suit is the foundation of the professional man's wardrobe.
- ◆ Effective shopping can be accomplished by making a list of needed items, allowing adequate time to shop, becoming familiar with clothing stores in your area, wearing the proper clothing while shopping, examining the quality of the garments you are considering, and purchasing classic styles.
- ◆ Proper fit is a result of clothes that are attractive and functional, are comfortable, and allow you to do your job during a normal workday.
- ◆ Wardrobe budget management can be mastered by knowing what you need to purchase, becoming familiar with the stores in you area, knowing the stores that have special purchasing agreements, knowing the best time of year to make purchases, purchasing quality items, and considering the cost and care of the items.
- ◆ Clothing requires attention to its care and maintenance. Clothing should always be repaired immediately and should be cleaned regularly. Clothing should be properly stored and be easy to access.

5
Manners and Etiquette for the Professional

AT THE CORE

This topic examines:

- ➤ THE IMPORTANCE OF MANNERS AND ETIQUETTE
- ➤ CUSTOMER SERVICE
- ➤ MAKING INTRODUCTIONS
- ➤ MAINTAINING CONVERSATIONS
- ➤ EATING AND DINING RULES
- ➤ GIFT-GIVING GUIDELINES
- ➤ IMPORTANCE OF PUNCTUALITY
- ➤ FOREIGN VISITORS AND PROTOCOL
- ➤ RESOURCES FOR MANNERS AND ETIQUETTE

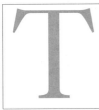

This module has emphasized that professional image is a component of many elements of appearance and behavior. You have learned that it is important to be well groomed and to dress appropriately to communicate a positive, professional image.

Another important aspect of professional image is how you interact with others in the business environment. Your interaction is required to perform many of the following functions:

- Communicate
- Dine with others
- Make introductions
- Express appreciation or condolences
- Give gifts
- Recognize the basics of foreign protocol

All of these are important aspects of the professional's ability to function in the business environment using correct manners and etiquette for each situation.

The Importance of Manners and Etiquette

Basic rules of etiquette represent a challenge for many professionals, but there is much to be learned from observing others and accessing resources that provide guidance on the proper course of action in various situations. After you learn and use proper manners and appropriate etiquette techniques, they become natural to you. Just like any other aspect of professional development, you must first know what is expected and then practice this on a regular basis. You can become comfortable with the use of proper manners, which will positively distinguish you from others in the business environment.

> *"Who needs a book of etiquette? Everyone does . . . for we must all learn socially acceptable ways of living."*
> **—Amy Vanderbilt**

Knowing and respecting others will identify you as a person who recognizes the diversity of others and the importance of manners to create a positive and civil work environment. There are common words that are universally accepted and appreciated. These include "please and thank you." In all situations, these are appropriate. In addition, understanding social expectations by using proper manners will help you develop a greater sense of self-confidence in a variety of settings. Nothing is more frustrating than not knowing what to do in a social setting. You can avoid this situation by trying to anticipate what the setting will be, asking others about the expectations, and researching the proper behavior and actions for the situation. It is important for you to recognize the significance of being at ease with the basic rules of manners and etiquette in a business environment. This can determine your upward mobility; the comfort of your customers; and your professional image among your peers, customers, and supervisors. Marie Betts-Johnson, president of International Protocol Institute of California, says, "Business etiquette is the key to confidence. We respect people through knowledge of etiquette and making them feel valuable."[1]

Customer Service

There are many rules of customer service that should be observed, and some are very specific to the profession in which you are working. However, many are universal and apply to all situations. It is important to recognize that you will have both internal and external customers. In other words, your customers are also the people with whom you work. These individuals deserve good customer service as they interact with you. Learn these basic rules, and practice them whenever you interact with customers.

- Always recognize and acknowledge the customer immediately.
- Listen carefully to what the customer is communicating to you.
- Accommodate the needs of the customer.
- Confirm the information you have received after listening carefully.
- Let the customer know what you can and cannot do to meet a request.
- Remain calm and polite regardless of the situation.
- Follow up and follow through with any actions that are required.

You should see in these basic rules a "circle" of actions. You begin with acknowledgment of the customer through a smile; shaking hands; answering the telephone; returning a telephone call; or sending correspondence such as an e-mail, a memo, or a letter. Do not keep people waiting unnecessarily. Even if you cannot give them the exact information they need immediately, you should let them know that you heard their request.

TIP Always make sure you follow up with a customer about any promised products or services.

The next phase of customer service is to listen to what the customer has requested or provided. This may mean being silent while he or she presents an issue, reading a memo carefully and picking out key points, or listening carefully to a telephone message. In all situations, you should attempt to accommodate the needs of the customer. The customer may sometimes request something you cannot provide, but you should never break company rules for a customer. Instead, you should explain to the customer what you can do and offer alternatives or solutions through appropriate means. In all instances, a professional stays calm and uses polite interaction with the customer. This can be challenging at times, as you encounter difficult, demanding customers. This is a true test of a professional. If you can remain calm while the customer is upset or rude, you have displayed a high level of professionalism.

The final aspect of the communications circle in customer service is to follow up and follow through. Once you promise a customer an action, you must follow up if you want to maintain your integrity with the customer. If a situation changes, you must keep the customer informed. Remember that good customer service is for both internal and external people. Positive customer relations are very important to your professional image and can be a significant distinguishing factor in your performance in the business environment.

Mary-Ellen Drummond, author and president of Polished Presentations International, suggests the following guidelines for exceptional customer service:

1. Observe and learn from good customer service.
2. Remember that customers and potential customers are all around you.
3. Set an example for employees by performing good customer service.
4. Provide and receive training to develop customer service skills.
5. Take time to practice good customer service.
6. Measure your effectiveness with your customers.
7. Implement a plan for improvement.
8. Do more than the customer expects.
9. Cultivate empathy through active listening.
10. Learn to express common phrases tactfully.
11. Deliver great customer service and earn customer loyalty.[2]

Making Introductions

Introductions may seem to be a tricky etiquette issue. However, one simple rule will help you with this important aspect of professional image. Remember to mention first the name of the person you consider the most important. For instance, if you are introducing your company CEO, Mr. Henry Johnson, to your new client, Ms. Carol Summers, you would mention the name of your company CEO first. You would say, "Mr. Johnson, I would like you to meet Ms. Summers." You might then add a small piece of information about one of the people to help get a con-

©PhotoDisc, Inc.

versation started. An example might be that both people are from the same city or both are fans of the same athletic team. Anything you add that provides a non-controversial beginning to an initial meeting is good. You are including a little background, which can help put people at ease during introductions.

> **TIP**   Always mention first the name of the person you want to honor the most when making introductions.

It may be difficult sometimes to determine who is most important. Susan Bixler, author of *Professional Presence*, suggests that when you "remember that you honor and give added recognition to the person who is first mentioned, introductions will be easy, connecting, and correct."[3] The most important thing to remember is to make the introduction. Usually, women are introduced to men and older people are introduced to younger people. Another helpful tip when making introductions or being introduced is to repeat the name of the people in the group so you can remember their names when you see them later. Also, if you are approaching someone and you know the person but you suspect he or she does not know who you are, by all means extend your hand and introduce yourself. A professional pays attention to these small details of etiquette so others feel comfortable during social situations.

Maintaining Conversations

As a professional, you are asked to interact with many people during the course of most business days. You must maintain business conversations as well as social conversations. You can develop your ability to carry on positive conversations that are enjoyed by everyone by keeping a few simple guidelines in mind as you interact with people.

- Make sure that everyone knows everyone else.
- Keep the conversation topic on something to which everyone can contribute.
- Listen carefully to what a person is saying.
- Try to involve others in conversation by asking questions or asking their opinion.
- Avoid topics that are controversial or that may be offensive to certain people.
- Do not interrupt others while they are speaking.
- Always conclude a conversation positively and express your pleasure at having talked with the individual.
- When conversing over a meal, avoid unpleasant or inappropriate topics.

The art of effective conversation is developed over a period of time with practice. However, most experts will tell you that the key to effective conversation is being genuinely interested in the other person. The other person needs to believe that your interest is sincere and that their input is valued. This is accomplished through active listening, courteous exchange of ideas, and positive body language such as smiles and appropriate laughter. Betts-Johnson recommends that you spend at least ten minutes with each person you meet to make a lasting connection.[4]

TIP Listening is an important aspect of maintaining an effective conversation.

Eating and Dining Rules

The business environment today may involve eating and dining engagements for the professional. Whether it is an informal luncheon, a cocktail party, or a formal dinner party, the professional needs to know the basics of dining etiquette to feel comfortable and confident in these situations. Again, some basic rules should be followed to make you feel comfortable and to ensure appropriate dining etiquette.

©PhotoDisc, Inc.

- Place your napkin in your lap as soon as you are seated.
- Look at the table setting to familiarize yourself with the place setting.
- Follow the lead of the host or hostess.
- Maintain good posture, and do not bend over your food. Food should be brought to the mouth for eating.
- Keep elbows off the table.
- Cut individual pieces of food with your fork holding the food while you cut with the knife.
- When eating soup, carry the spoon away from the bowl and then to your mouth.
- Leave your utensils on your plate between bites of food. The knife should be placed at the top of the plate horizontally with the blade away from you.
- When finished eating, place the utensils parallel to each other at the top of the plate. This alerts the server that you have finished your meal.
- If you are eating bread, break off a piece of the bread first. Do not bite into the entire piece of bread, and never butter the entire piece of bread. Butter is applied to one piece of bread at a time with your individual butter knife or dinner knife. Never use the serving knife to butter your bread.
- If you drop a utensil, leave it on the floor; ask the server for another.
- Use the utensils in the order they are presented to you at the place setting. Start from the outside, and work toward your plate. Salad forks are usually smaller than dinner forks. You can also find dessert forks or spoons placed above the plate.
- Lay your napkin in your chair when you leave the table and plan to return.

TIP The business meal can be a time to build networks, get to know customers, and enhance your role in your organization if you know how to conduct yourself appropriately.

If you are a host, you want to follow some additional dining rules to make your guest(s) feel comfortable.

- Arrive early so your guest(s) are not kept waiting.
- Select foods that are easy to eat and that create the least amount of challenge to consume.
- Place your napkin in your lap as soon as you sit down.
- Allow your guest(s) to select their food first when serving as the host for a meal.
- Offer suggestions for food if the restaurant is unfamiliar to your guest(s).
- Tell the server immediately who is to receive the check or if separate checks are required.
- If you would like to order an appetizer, alcohol, or a dessert, or think your guest(s) would like to do so, indicate that this is acceptable.

If you are the guest at a meal function, follow these basic rules in addition to the previous dining rules presented.

- Follow your host's lead in ordering food.
- Inquire about which foods are good or if the restaurant has a specialty.
- Select foods that are easy to consume and that represent the fewest challenges.
- Select moderately priced foods to avoid extremes.
- Do not order an appetizer, alcohol, or a dessert unless everyone else does.
- Try to pace your food consumption along with that of your host. You do not want to finish too soon or too late.
- Thank your host for the meal, and offer reciprocity at a later date.

It is important that you learn and practice these basic rules of dining etiquette so you are comfortable when using them. Bixler suggests the following tips to help make any business dining experience a positive one:

- Don't take too much time reviewing the menu. This could indicate indecisiveness.
- Don't take medication at the table.

- Refrain from too much conversation with the waitperson.
- Avoid selecting the same thing as another guest.
- Stay away from soup, pasta, messy foods such as hamburgers, or any food you must eat with your fingers.
- Don't rush from one topic to another.
- Ensure quality service for everyone at the table if you are the host.
- Order the same progression of food as your guests so they will not be eating alone.
- As host or hostess, you should always order last.
- Handle the bill and tip quietly and quickly.[5]

In addition to dining etiquette, the professional may be called upon to interact with others during cocktail parties or business social occasions. You should follow the general rules of conversation presented earlier in this section. Also remember that these situations are for the purpose of mixing and mingling, where eating and drinking is not a priority. The well-respected professional recognizes the importance of developing networks and interacting socially with others. This may be difficult to do with both a plate of food and a drink in your hands. Therefore, keep the objective of networking as your primary reason to attend these functions.

Gift-Giving Guidelines

There will be occasions when you want to remember a customer, peer, or supervisor with a gift. A well-selected and appropriate gift can communicate many messages that will help you in the business environment. When selecting a gift for someone, provide something that is appropriate for the occasion and that sends the appropriate message. For instance, you would select a different gift for someone grieving the loss of a loved one than for someone celebrating the birth of a child. You might send a floral arrangement or a small book of inspirations to someone who has experienced a loss.

For a younger professional, you might select an item that would be useful to him or her in the workplace. Whatever the situation, you need to determine what you want to accomplish by giving the gift. Generally in the workplace, you are trying to be thoughtful of a co-workers' situation, not trying to impress him or her with costly gifts. A customer may appreciate a hand-delivered copy of your new company catalog with a thoughtful note attached about how much you appreciate his or her business. Gift giving is also sometimes done as a group in the business environment. If you want to participate in this type of activity, contribute what you think you can without straining your budget. If you are unable to contribute, quietly let the person who is in charge of the activity know that you would like to decline. One of the most thoughtful gifts given in the business world today is a handwritten note. Other ideas for business gift giving include the following:

- Small dish garden for the desk
- Book of inspiration
- Gift certificate to a restaurant
- Photograph frame
- Calendar
- Basket of fruit
- Desk nameplate
- Stamp holder
- Business card holder

Susan Bixler says, "Thoughtful, appropriate gift giving reveals an elegance, a savvy, and a sense of good breeding that are very important to business."[6]

Importance of Punctuality

A professional recognizes the importance of being punctual. This simple characteristic communicates your value of other people's time. Make it a habit to be a punctual and prompt individual who follows up and follows through. An aspect of punctuality that is highly regarded in both professional and social environments involves the acknowledgment of an invitation. You will be expected to let the person who is hosting an external meeting or social event know whether you plan to attend. This is known as "RSVP." Whenever you receive an invitation, check your calendar for availability and respond immediately if you are unable to attend. This is a common courtesy and should be followed at all times. You should be aware that plans for meals, seating, and planned activities are made based on the number of persons attending the event. Once you have acknowledged your attendance, you should be at the event. The only valid reason for not attending after accepting would be one of a serious nature and unavoidable.

The individuals with whom you interact will expect meetings to start on time, deadlines on projects to be met, and actions to be completed. A professional makes sure that he or she is organized and prepared for meetings, arrives at appointments a few minutes prior to the appointed time, and meets with customers at scheduled times. This shows respect for others and the demands that are made upon their time. Anytime you cannot keep an appointment or arrive at a meeting in a timely manner, the other person(s) waiting on you should be notified immediately about the delay. This is a common courtesy of a professional. You want to avoid the habit of being habitually late and becoming known for this.

Foreign Visitors and Protocol

The world has become a much smaller place in which we all work because of telecommunications and technology. You will probably conduct business with many different people from a variety of international backgrounds in the course of your professional life. Volumes have been written about the specifics of conducting business in certain cultures and countries around the world. If you work for a company that conducts a substantial amount of business with other countries, you will probably be schooled extensively on the specifics unique to that country. In such a case, you must become very familiar with the guidelines for conducting business with that culture.

Most professionals interact in a more general nature and should
follow general rules of protocol applicable to most environments.

- Avoid any prototyping of people from other cultures.
- Take the time to learn about the cultures of the people with whom
  you work.
- Be sensitive to the customs and practices of others.
- Address others with a title and their last name to avoid too much
  familiarity.
- Use common courtesy terms frequently, such as "please" and "thank
  you."
- Display patience while dealing with people from other cultures, as
  Americans tend to communicate they are always in a hurry.
- Demonstrate your attentiveness to the comfort and well-being of
  your guest(s).
- Identify some topics of conversation that are non-controversial so
  you can carry on a conversation with people from other cultures.
- Avoid slang and jargon while conversing, as this may not be under-
  stood.

This aspect of professional development represents a challenge
for most individuals. However, it is one that can be learned and mastered by making it a priority. Your objective as a professional should be
to make others feel comfortable and welcome in your environment.

Resources for Manners and Etiquette

Most people have plenty to learn about manners and etiquette.
Some people have been taught these basics; others have not been so
fortunate. However, numerous resources are available to help develop
this component of your professional image. Some of these include:

- Mentors—They observe what others are doing and how they are
  doing it.

- Magazines and periodicals—Many printed sources are available that offer short articles on professional manners and etiquette. These can be very helpful to you as a professional.
- Books—Entire books deal with manners and etiquette, ranging from informal settings to very formal functions. Investing in a basic etiquette book is a good idea for an upcoming professional who wants to develop his or her skills in this area. There are also publications on the specifics of business etiquette that would be helpful to any professional.
- Online resources—The Internet offers a variety of resources for information regarding professional image as it relates to manners and etiquette. There are sites that provide interactive exchanges so people can ask and receive answers to their questions.

As a professional, you must know how to interact with people and what to do in certain social situations. As a professional, you need to give this your attention so you are ready to meet the challenges in this area of your image development.

RECAP OF KEY CONCEPTS

- Proficiency in the use of manners and etiquette is very important in your professional image development.
- You must be able to communicate, dine with others, make introductions, express appreciation or condolences, give gifts, and recognize the basics of foreign protocol.
- Focusing on the needs of your customers and clients results in effective customer relations.
- When making introductions, you should first mention the name of the person you want to honor the most.
- When maintaining conversations, you should listen carefully, avoid interrupting, and conclude your conversation positively.
- It is important to learn basic dining protocol so you are comfortable while entertaining guests or being a guest.
- The objective of gift gifting is to recognize the needs of the person to whom you are giving the gift. A gift does not need to be expensive, but it should be appropriate.
- A professional recognizes the importance of punctuality and respects the time of others.
- Foreign protocol requires that you pay special attention to the needs of your guests. You should learn about the customs of people from other cultures with whom you interact.
- Several resources are available to assist you in developing your manners and etiquette expertise. These include mentors, magazines and periodicals, books, and online resources.

6
Personal Behavior

AT THE CORE
This topic examines:

➤ **THE PROFESSIONAL AS A ROLE MODEL**

➤ **ASSUMING RESPONSIBILITY**

➤ **RESPECTING DIVERSITY**

➤ **HANDLING CONFLICT AND CHANGE**

➤ **MAINTAINING APPROPRIATE RELATIONSHIPS WITH COWORKERS**

➤ **ETHICAL BUSINESS PRACTICES**

➤ **MAINTAINING CONFIDENTIALITY**

s an individual, you should recognize the significance of your professional image as it relates to you personally and as it represents your company. In a professional role, you not only communicate messages about yourself but also communicate messages about your organization or company. This becomes increasingly important as you interact with the public and with customers as a representative of your organization. The general public does not separate you from the company when they speak with you, receive a letter from you, or observe your behavior in different settings.

The Professional as a Role Model

Your personal behavior is representative of the organization's accepted behavior in the minds of the customer and the general public. You are the company to the customer. Therefore, it is very important for you to recognize this role and your responsibility as you conduct yourself in the presence of customers and the general public. If you demonstrate an intolerance of diversity or impatience with a customer, the customer may interpret this behavior to be the position of the organization. The old saying "Actions speak a thousand words" captures the essence of the importance of the personal behavior of a professional.

In addition to representing your organization, your personal behavior may also affect your upward mobility in an organization. Employers look for professionals who are responsible in their personal actions and who recognize the consequences of failing to meet certain standards of behavior. Advancement in your profession depends on how well you are able to assume responsibility, respect diversity, handle conflicts, take criticism, conduct business in an ethical and honest manner, and continue to learn and develop as an employee. All of these areas represent an opportunity for you to display maturity and responsibility in your role as a professional.

Assuming Responsibility

As a professional, probably nothing separates you from others more than the ability to accept responsibility for your job, your actions, and the consequences of failing to fulfill obligations. Responsibility in your professional role has many aspects that you need to understand and accept as a part of the job. First, it is your responsibility to learn about your job and the duties associated with your position. A professional does not wait for someone to tell him or her about every aspect of the job. You must take the initiative to determine the scope of your position while still staying within the parameters of your authority. It is important to identify how your position fits into the mission of the organization and what is expected of you in your job performance. You can accomplish this by reviewing your job description, talking with your supervisor, reviewing files and information about your area within the organization, and talking with coworkers. However, the most important connection you have with your position should come through your supervisor and a focus on the mission of the organization or your work unit.

> **TIP**   Responsibility means doing your job the right way and doing it on time without someone having to tell you to do it.

Responsibility also involves taking action for fulfilling the job duties in a quality manner. The quality of your work is a reflection of your personal and professional performance. A professional is always aware of the significance of producing quality work so it reflects positively on the organization. In addition, your work is usually a component of a much larger product; therefore, it is important for you to contribute quality input. If your work is not accurate or timely, it may delay a project or result in work being completed again. Timeliness and accuracy of work reflects a commitment to your job responsibilities.

Another important aspect of professional responsibility is the ability to accept the consequences of your failing to fulfill an obligation. For instance, if you have not submitted work in a timely or accurate manner or if you have failed to acquire adequate knowledge about your job duties, you must acknowledge this to your supervisor and determine what you can do to improve the situation and avoid this mistake in the future. A real professional is respected in the workplace when he or she can admit a mistake and accept responsibility for failures as well as successes. If you have the unfortunate experience of making a serious mistake, you should inform your supervisor immediately. This applies to both internal and external issues. It is always better for your supervisor to hear about a situation from you rather than another source.

Respecting Diversity

In the diverse and global work environment that now exists, it is very important for a professional to respect all people. Diversity is a complex issue that requires tolerance, respect, and knowledge of others. A professional is mindful of his or her behavior and communications as they relate to diversity. Even though others may be different from you in gender, race, or ethnic background, everyone can make a positive contribution in the workplace and should be respected for his or her role in the accomplishment of the mission of the organization.

Professionals resist the impulse to judge people solely on their appearance or gender. Professionals respect people for their individual selves and do not allow preconceived ideas about certain groups to affect the manner in which they work with others. It may be a difficult exercise to look at yourself and determine if you have prejudices that interfere with your ability to communicate and work effectively with others; however, you need to do so in order to be more effective in the work environment.

> **TIP** The workplace is an increasingly diverse environment that requires tolerance for everyone's differences.

Failure to respect diversity is a barrier to productivity and can contribute to poor working conditions. As a professional, you should refrain from making hasty judgments about people based on gender, race, or ethnic background. You should refrain from making comments or jokes about groups of people, as this may be offensive to others. You must work on being an open-minded and tolerant person. This not only will contribute to your ability to work effectively in your profession but also will earn you a high degree of respect among the people with whom you work.

Handling Conflict and Change

Regardless of how well an organization functions, there will be periods of conflict or change that test your professionalism.

Conflict. Conflict can bring out the very worst or the very best in a professional. Conflict can be a result of a simple misunderstanding, or it can be the result of a major situation within an organization. It is important to maintain a calm demeanor and control your emotions during periods of conflict. You should recognize that there are times during a conflict when it is important *not* to say what is on your mind. Silence can be important during a conflict. Consider the repercussions of being too frank or revealing too much. This certainly does not mean you should be untruthful or withhold information that is important, but it also does not mean you can say everything you feel. It is important to recognize when you are angry and to decide that perhaps you should not speak up about an issue. This may save you many hours of regret. Being able to control your anger is important in your professional image development.

TIP   When a conflict does not directly involve you, stay out of it.

Exercising Restraint. When a conflict does not directly involve you, it is better to stay out of the situation. If you are viewed as a person who is constantly involved in conflicts in the workplace, it may be to the detriment of your career. Employers are looking for professionals who know how to exercise judgment and restraint in involving themselves in situations and who contribute to the overall effectiveness of the workplace through their professional behavior.

This is especially true when you refrain from engaging in inappropriate conversation or gossip in your office. Remember that most people go through difficult times in their personal and professional lives at some time or another. If what you know or hear about a person cannot contribute positively to his or her image, be a professional and be quiet!

There is a difference in listening to the office grapevine to learn about internal issues and being a malicious gossip. You want to stay away from the latter. Bixler suggests that even though the company manual does not identify who to stay away from, you should get smart and listen in. She maintains that the office grapevine is usually 80 percent accurate, so there may be some valuable information to be learned by listening.[1]

TIP   The winds of change are constantly blowing in today's business environment.

As a professional, it is important to remember that things constantly change in the business world. As a result, you must be willing to change with the situation. Today's work environment is one of global competition in which technology affects the way in which work is completed. You must be willing to embrace change for the positive results it can bring. Certainly not all change is good, but most companies do not pursue change with the intent of failure. Changes esult in different work environments and different organizational structures. Changes in organizational structure can be difficult for people to accept and manage; however, you will be setting yourself apart from others if you commit yourself to being open-minded about changes and are willing to work in a new environment. You will be recognized as a person who has the ability to support organizational changes to ensure the vitality of an organization.

Maintaining Appropriate Relationships with Coworkers

An important aspect of professional behavior involves your ability to maintain appropriate relationships in the work environment. This means you should always have a professional relationship with your coworkers. It is not appropriate to date people from your immediate work area. There should also be a limit to the type of personal relationship you develop with your supervisor or someone you supervise. This can cause a variety of problems in the workplace even under the best of circumstances and has the potential of being a professional disaster if the relationship does not go well. Some of the problems that can develop involve the perception of others that you may be receiving or granting unfair advantage because of the relationship. This will limit your ability to manage others and will greatly diminish your respectability in the work environment.

> **TIP**   A professional's goal is to maintain his or her personal life outside of his or her professional life.

Managing Your Personal Life.   Another aspect of maintaining appropriate relationships is your ability to manage your personal life outside of the work environment. Your personal life should remain personal and not be brought to work with you. Everyone has serious personal situations at one time or another, but it is important to try to maintain a distance between your personal and professional roles. Find someone with whom you can share concerns and get honest feedback about a situation, preferably someone outside of your work environment. You never know when the person in whom you have confided will share information that could hurt you personally or professionally.

It is unfortunate but true that people sometimes make professional judgments based on personal information. Examples of personal situations that should remain private include details about marriages, children, personal health, and financial circumstances. The fewer details that are shared about these situations at work, the better. You may even be faced with a colleague who inquires about a personal situation. As a professional, you have several options in this type of situation. You can tell the colleague that you do not discuss personal situations, or you can provide general information. An example of an appropriate response regarding a family matter might be a statement such as "I am facing a serious situation in my family and am working through it. I appreciate your concern and respect for my privacy." This type of response should satisfy most people and still maintain your privacy. You should also respect the privacy of others and refrain from gossiping or making inappropriate inquiries about their personal situations. Inappropriate communication about people and work can contribute negatively to a professional environment. You must develop an ability to respect the decisions of management as they make changes, and you should respect the privacy of others who may be experiencing personal difficulties. This means not talking unnecessarily or speculating about actions or situations.

Appropriate Office Protocol. You should also respect your coworkers by refraining from asking them to purchase items from you, borrow money, or contribute to activities that may not be of interest to them. The office is no place to solicit for your children's activities regardless of how worthy the cause. People may ask to purchase items from you, but they should not be approached. It is never appropriate to ask a coworker about borrowing money. Everyone has occasionally borrowed change for the vending machine, but you do not demonstrate professionalism when you fail to have money when going out to lunch or when you fail to contribute an appropriate tip when dining out with a group. If you have agreed to contribute to a gift for someone, then you should make your contribution in a timely manner. On the other hand, you have the right to decline participation if this is more appropriate for your situation. You should also respect others who may decline to participate in giving a gift or taking part in a social activity.

When borrowing items from others in the office, make sure you return them. If you use someone's stapler or paper shredder, return it in a timely manner and in good working condition. It is important to respect other's property. This means that you do not use other people's property or their items without permission. You demonstrate your respect for others in the workplace by "pulling your weight" in a variety of situations. This may mean that you take the initiative to clean up the break room, replenish supplies in a conference room, or make coffee when the need arises. Also, when someone has helped you on a project, try to find a way to help when he or she needs assistance. Reciprocity is important to facilitate good working relationships in the business world. More importantly, if someone declines an offer to participate in an activity, respect his or her decision.

Ethical Business Practices

Your professional reputation is one to be guarded carefully and should receive your utmost attention as you develop personal and professional practices for conducting business.

You must always be honest and ethical in business transactions. Customers expect this when they conduct business with you, and your coworkers expect this with all internal dealings. You must be honest with people by providing them with accurate and timely information. Lying is never acceptable. If you cannot meet a deadline with a customer, you must inform the customer of this; the customer can then determine the appropriate course of action. If a product you sell cannot accomplish a certain task, you must be honest about this fact. Most people do not mind being informed that a deadline cannot be met or that a product cannot perform in a certain manner; however, they usually resent very much being mislead about a timeline or an action.

Internally you must submit accurate records for reimbursement of work performed. Failure to do so could lead to a reprimand or a dismissal. Expense accounts should be used for business only, not for personal transactions. It is important to use the facilities at work for work only. This means limiting your time on the telephone for personal business to an absolute minimum. You should never take supplies from the office for personal use. As a professional, you should take sick leave when you are actually ill and not because you want a day off. You should give advance notice when you need to take leave from your job, and you should try to schedule vacation during times when it does not create an undue hardship on others. A professional recognizes the importance of maintaining completely honest and ethical practices.

Maintaining Confidentiality

As a professional, you should recognize and maintain the confidentiality of all business that is conducted by your employer. There are both internal and external confidentiality issues to recognize in your role as an employee. Internally you must communicate only with those people who have a reason to know about the nature of the transactions in your work area. Do not make the mistake of thinking that just because someone works for your company, you can reveal confidential information to him or her. You must take responsibility for maintaining your work area, including your computer files, so people who do not need to know this information cannot access it. You should exercise caution in disposing of confidential materials in your wastebasket. Some items should be shredded (for example, information regarding salaries or personnel actions such as reprimands or terminations). Files should not be left in view of others even when in your office. Before meetings in your office, you should make sure that any confidential material is put away so it cannot be seen or accessed. You must also exercise caution when making copies of confidential materials. Do not casually throw away copies of information because of poor copy quality. Documents can be taken from the trash or recycling bin and read. You must be careful to discuss information in a confidential environment on the telephone or in your office with the door closed. You also should not discuss salary, compensation, or evaluation issues with anyone other than your supervisor. This is a very important aspect of confidentiality.

External confidentiality is also important. You cannot discuss company issues with your family members or friends. You never know what relationships may exist outside the work environment that may adversely affect company business if you share information. The financial condition of your organization, its policies and procedures, or any challenges that are occurring in your business should not be discussed. The names of customers should not be disclosed or discussed in any manner. You must exercise extreme caution in this area in case someone approaches you about a customer or client. Your response should always be "I do not discuss any business whatsoever outside of my job." Failure to recognize this very important aspect of confidentiality can lead to serious problems in your professional life. Remember, you would not want someone to be discussing your financial, personal, or medical issues with others. Give this same respect to your customers and clients.

RECAP OF KEY CONCEPTS

- You represent your company in your professional role, and customers do not distinguish you from the company.
- You must learn about your job responsibilities. You must take the initiative to fulfill your job duties. You must accept responsibility for your mistakes.
- Diversity requires tolerance, respect, and knowledge of others. Even though others may be different from you in gender, race, or ethnic background, everyone can make a positive contribution in the workplace and should be respected for his or her role in the accomplishment of the mission of the organization.
- A professional is careful when involved in a conflict to get all the facts, listen to the issues, and know when to refrain from becoming involved. When things change in your organization, you want to be accepting and accommodating by communicating your support.
- It is important to maintain appropriate relationships in the workplace. This means that you do not date or become romantically involved with people in your immediate work area or with people you supervise or who supervise you.
- A professional should keep his or her personal life out of the workplace.
- You should respect the privacy and property of your coworkers.
- It is important to develop a professional image that communicates your high standards of integrity, honesty, and trustworthiness.
- Confidentiality is an important responsibility of a professional and should be maintained at all times.

7
Communicating Professionally

AT THE CORE
This topic examines:

➤ **SPEAKING CORRECTLY**

➤ **WRITTEN COMMUNICATIONS**

➤ **EXPRESSING APPRECIATION**

➤ **EFFECTIVE LISTENING**

➤ **COMMUNICATING INTERNALLY**

➤ **COMMUNICATING EXTERNALLY**

➤ **COMMUNICATING IN DIFFICULT SITUATIONS**

The ability to communicate effectively is critical to your development as a professional. Your expertise at speaking correctly, writing effectively, expressing appreciation, listening effectively, and communicating appropriately will contribute positively to your professional image and upward mobility in your profession. Communication skills are developed through the practice of effective techniques and the ability to determine how well you communicate with others. Continuous assessment of communication skills and effectiveness is key to the refinement of these skills.

You will be required to communicate both internally and externally in your profession. Internally you will communicate with coworkers and supervisors; externally you will communicate with customers and clients. Improving communication skills is important as you develop your professional image because employers recognize the importance of hiring employees who are effective communicators. Employers understand how critical accurate, timely, and appropriate communication can be to their organization.

Speaking Correctly

Being able to speak correctly is a basic communication skill you must possess to work effectively with others and to advance in your profession. A high percentage of communication that occurs in the business environment involves some form of oral communication.

©Eyewire

This can range from a simple greeting to a coworker to an extended telephone conference with a client. Speaking correctly involves many components including the following:

- Using appropriate diction
- Using correct English
- Avoiding slang and acronyms
- Speaking with confidence
- Communicating with clarity, conciseness, and accuracy

Using Appropriate Diction. Diction is defined as "the manner of expression in words and the choice of words as well as enunciation." You should strive to select words that clearly communicate your message, and you must enunciate and pronounce those words in a manner that projects them from your mouth to the listener. This involves facing your listener while you are speaking, pronouncing each word individually, and completing the pronunciation of the word without dropping the ending. These techniques will contribute to your use of appropriate diction.

Using Correct English. Another aspect of speaking correctly involves the use of correct English. It is important that you use proper English in oral as well as written communication. You should make sure when you speak that subjects and verbs agree and that pronouns agree in number and gender.

Avoiding Slang and Acronyms. Avoid using slang even in casual conversation, as this may become a habit in your formal conversations. Slang can also be offensive to some people, which is reason enough to avoid its use. You should also avoid the overuse of acronyms when communicating externally. Even though you may know what these acronyms mean, the person with whom you are communicating may not and may feel intimidated because he or she does not know what you are talking about.

Speaking with Confidence. Speaking with confidence involves knowing your subject matter, interacting with the listener, and delivering the message in an understandable form. Your confidence as a speaker increases as your knowledge of the subject increases; therefore, you should be prepared and knowledgeable about your subject. This is applicable even in informal settings. If you are speaking with your supervisor about a problem in production, then you should investigate the situation and be prepared to present the facts. Your interaction with the listener is important; you must try to determine if the listener is receiving your message as you intended. This involves listening actively, observing reactions, and verifying the message given.

> **TIP** The secret to speaking with confidence is knowing your subject and practicing your delivery.

Communicating with Clarity, Conciseness, and Accuracy. The last aspect of developing confidence as a speaker involves your ability to deliver the message in understandable terms. For most communication, you should deliver a simple message that offers the listener clarity. Avoid the extra words or introduction that may interfere with your message. You should avoid hesitant expressions such as "ah," "uh," and "ok," as these terms tend to indicate less confidence. Communication should always be clear, concise, and accurate. When speaking with someone in person, always remember to:

- Maintain eye contact.
- Face the person so your words are projected toward the listener.
- Watch for the reaction of the listener.
- Verify what you have said if there is any question about the message.
- Ask for questions from the listener.
- Make a notation about any follow-up that is required.

Telephone Guidelines. A significant oral communication medium in the business world today is the telephone. As a professional, you are expected to communicate effectively on the telephone with coworkers and customers.

Observe the following guidelines for effective verbal communication on the telephone:

- Answer your own telephone whenever possible.
- Always return calls the same day, if possible.
- Have someone keep your callers informed about your availability.
- Respect others' time when placing calls, and determine if it is a good time for the person to talk with you.
- Speak clearly into the telephone.
- Do not eat or drink while on the telephone.
- When leaving messages, indicate the best time for a return call.
- Avoid the use of cellular telephones in meetings unless absolutely necessary.

Professionals are sometimes called upon to make internal presentations to their coworkers or external presentations to customers and clients. The ability to develop a presentation topic and deliver the message is a requirement of many professional positions within organizations. Expertise in this area is developed through practice and experience. If you have an opportunity to give presentations to small internal groups, take advantage of these situations; they can provide the opportunity for you to develop your skills. Select a person you trust in the group, and get feedback from that person on your delivery, presentation media content, and overall effectiveness of the presentation. You should develop your public speaking skills as well as your one-on-one communication skills. Many of the same techniques apply to larger groups as for one-on-one communication.

> **TIP**   You will become more at ease with oral presentations through practice, experience, and assessment.

Oral Presentation Guidelines. General guidelines for developing your ability to make oral presentations are as follows:

- Determine exactly how much time you have for your presentation.
- Select the best medium for delivery.
- Identify the key points you want to communicate.
- Practice your presentation.
- Be familiar with any equipment used.
- Get feedback from someone in the group after your presentation.
- Critique yourself for improvement.

Even though you may not like giving presentations initially, you can develop your skills in this area. If you become proficient as a speaker both to individuals and to groups of people, you will contribute significantly to your professional image.

Written Communications

In written communications, you must focus on clarity, conciseness, and accuracy for the reader to interpret your message correctly. As a professional, you will be required to compose a variety of written communications. These include memos, e-mails, letters, reports, and proposals. The primary objective of most business communication is conciseness. Effective business communication does not require extra wording, as most readers want the message in a clear and concise manner. Therefore, developing your ability to write effectively is important. Many tools are available to help you develop your writing skills; these include both electronic and traditional tools. All written communications should contain correct grammar, sentence structure, punctuation, spelling, and formatting.

©*PhotoDisc, Inc.*

Writing Guidelines. Specific guidelines for writing effective memos, e-mails, and reports are as follows:

Memos
- Identify your main point, and communicate this in the first paragraph.
- Limit the memo to one page.
- Personalize where possible and if appropriate.
- Spell check and proofread carefully prior to distributing.

E-mail
- Use e-mail for informal communication within the organization.
- Remember that e-mail is considered official communication and can be used in court as communicating the position of an organization.
- Be courteous and polite while using online communications.
- Keep e-mail brief.
- Spell check and proofread prior to distributing.

Reports
- Identify the purpose of the report.
- Inform the reader of how the report can be used.
- Make the report as brief as possible.
- Use a format that is easy to read and follow and allows the reader to locate information easily. (For example, use a table of contents or an index if the report is lengthy.)
- Use charts and tables to consolidate and compare data where appropriate.
- Check for accuracy and completeness of data throughout the report.
- Spell check and proofread before distributing.

Expressing Appreciation

A professional must be able to express appreciation to others who have assisted, accommodated, or extended some kindness. Appreciation can be expressed orally or in writing or sometimes both ways. The professional who graciously and appropriately expresses appreciation can distinguish himself or herself in the work environment. The most important aspect of expressing appreciation is realizing that it is an important component of professional image and responsibility. Sometimes people fail to recognize the importance of expressing appreciation and overlook this very simple but important aspect of professionalism.

> **TIP**   Two simple, powerful words—*Thank you*—can positively affect your professional image.

Very few people have gotten where they are in the business world without the help of others. You have many opportunities to extend appreciation to people; for example, when they:

- Served as a reference for a job.
- Gave you an opportunity to work in an area that is unfamiliar to you.
- Allowed you to participate on a work team or make a presentation.
- Provided assistance to you during a peak time or an important project.
- Provided professional advice or counseling.
- Recommended you for a promotion.
- Gave you a gift for a special occasion.
- Extended a kindness during a difficult time in your personal or professional life.

In each of these situations, the person who extended the accommodation to you should be acknowledged. When the person is extending the accommodation, he or she should be thanked verbally if at all possible. As a follow-up to a verbal expression of appreciation, you should write a short note of gratitude to the person, expressing how much you appreciate what he or she did and how it helped you. The note should be written from a personal standpoint, expressing appreciation for the kindness. You should invest in plain quality-paper note cards with your initials or with a simple businesslike border.

Special Acknowledgments.   As important as it is to acknowledge appreciation to others who have helped you, it is just as important to acknowledge occasions in other people's lives that affect them. For instance, when a coworker has experienced the death of a family member or is experiencing a difficult time caring for a parent, you might send a card or note saying you are thinking about him or her.

You have many ways to acknowledge someone in an appropriate manner. Some of these include sending a card; offering to run an errand; offering to work a shift or extra time for him or her; or sending a floral arrangement, a book, or a gift certificate for a product or service that would help the person. Remember, it is not the cost of the gift that is important; rather, if it is the acknowledgement of the other person's need to be remembered. You must maintain a business relationship and not cross too far into someone's personal life, but this does not mean that you cannot let a person know that you care and are concerned during a difficult time in his or her life.

Effective Listening

An often-overlooked aspect of effective communications is the art of listening. Listening is an aspect of communication that must be mastered to fully develop effective communication skills. Listening is an art! Stephen Covey states in his book *The 7 Habits of Highly Effective People* that we have not been taught to be good listeners. He goes deeper into this concept by proposing that we never can truly understand a person or his or her message until we learn to listen effectively. He states that through our communication with others, we demonstrate an understanding of the person and the message, and then trust and comfort are realized.[1]

People who know how to listen are usually excellent communicators and relate well to people. Listening involves understanding what is being said and what is not being said. Listening communicates that you are concerned about the total communication cycle. People feel your interest and, therefore, are more open to hearing what you have to say. A good listener usually has highly developed interpersonal skills and strong working relationships with coworkers and customers. You can learn what a customer wants and needs by allowing time for him or her to talk without interruption. The information you gather while listening can help you better serve your team members, coworkers, and customers.

Listening Guidelines. To become a better listener, follow these helpful guidelines.

- Recognize the importance of listening in the communication cycle.
- Give your full attention to the speaker.
- Try to follow the thoughts presented by the speaker.
- Do not interrupt the speaker until he or she has finished.
- Confirm what you think you have heard by verifying information with the speaker.
- Be aware of body language that may signal other meanings.

Listening is important and should receive your attention in your development as a professional.

Communicating Internally

You will have many opportunities to communicate internally with coworkers, supervisors, and other members of your organization. You will have reasons to communicate with others in meetings, in one-on-one situations with your supervisor, and with customers through a variety of methods. It is important to learn the accepted protocols for communication within your organization.

Your supervisor will expect communication from you regarding the status of projects and work assignments. You should plan what you want to say to your supervisor so meetings regarding the status of work in progress are efficient. If previous tasks require follow-up, you should have information readily accessible regarding these tasks. You should be prepared to share information with your supervisor regarding any challenges you anticipate with projects or in working with people. It is important to bring suggested solutions for problems and challenges to your supervisor. He or she will respect your initiative regarding problem solving if you adopt this approach. You should also provide timely responses to any internal communication. This will require that you read your correspondence, memos, and e-mail on a regular basis.

> **TIP** Failure to follow the chain of command can result in conflicts in the business environment.

Chain of Command. Another aspect of internal communications involves respecting the chain of command in your organization. Your supervisor will expect you to come to him or her with problems and concerns before going to a higher level. This is important in developing a positive working relationship with your supervisor. If you and your supervisor are having a dispute regarding your status as an employee, you may need to work with the personnel department of your organization. However, you still need to include your supervisor in the process by informing him or her that the communication is occurring. The only exception to keeping your supervisor informed of communication with the personnel department would be a situation in which you suspected dishonest practices within the organization. This type of situation requires direct communication with the personnel or security departments of your organization.

Group Communications. When communicating in meetings you should arrive at the meeting in a timely manner, be prepared for the purpose of the meeting, participate in the meeting, and make notation of any follow-up required. During the meeting, you should allow others to speak and contribute to the purpose of the meeting as well as make your own contributions. Listen carefully to what others have to say, and participate as a problem-solver in challenging situations.

Communicating Externally

When communicating with customers, it is important to provide clear and concise information about what you can provide to them. Whenever changes occur in production or in services, you should keep the customer informed. You should maintain frequent communication with your customers and clients to determine if their needs have changed and how your organization's products and/or services can meet those needs. You also determine the level of satisfaction of your customers and if their needs are not being met. This is an aspect of continuous improvement that most organizations are focused on in order to remain competitive in the work environment. Customers should always receive timely follow-ups to requests and inquiries, regardless of the mode of communication. E-mails, letters, and telephone calls from customers require immediate follow-up from you to acknowledge their receipt. This contributes to positive customer relations for your organization.

Communicating in Difficult Situations

All organizations experience difficult situations in which your expertise as a communicator may be challenged. Difficult communication situations can come from a variety of sources. Most of the time they are a result of miscommunication or people not meeting their obligations and responsibilities. Sometimes mistakes occur and are unavoidable. In any of these situations, you must accept responsibility for solving the problem and addressing the issue. When an apology is in order to a coworker, supervisor, or customer, you should do so immediately and work at preventing a repeat of the situation in the future.

As a professional, you want to determine what caused the mistake so it does not occur again. When dealing with a customer, you must determine whether your organization needs to provide additional recourse in correcting a problem. Of course, this needs to be completed within the policies of your organization and may require your supervisor's assistance. Interestingly, you will find that most people are willing to accept a sincere apology and move on in the working relationship. Learn from your mistakes, and realize that mistakes happen to everyone at one time or another. You are a true professional when you can recognize a mistake, acknowledge it to the people involved, and learn from your mistake.

TIP   Knowing when not to say anything is a significant communication tool.

Difficult situations that are not the result of a mistake sometimes arise. You may find that a customer or coworker is wrong in his or her approach to or stance on an issue because he or she does not understand the situation or refuses to acknowledge himself or herself as the party who is wrong. This type of situation requires a high level of expertise and professionalism in handling. You may need to acknowledge that you do not necessarily agree with the person, but you will try to resolve the issue. You may also have to accept that the individual will never acknowledge his or her position as being wrong. You should know when to say or *not* say something in a difficult situation. Sometimes silence is the solution to a difficult situation.

Remaining calm and courteous is always appropriate and projects a professional image.

RECAP OF KEY CONCEPTS

- Effective communication is critical to your development as a professional.
- You will be required to communicate both internally and externally in your professional role.
- Speaking correctly involves using appropriate diction, using correct English; avoiding slang and acronyms; speaking with confidence; and communicating with clarity, conciseness, and accuracy.
- When speaking to someone, maintain eye contact, face the person to project your words toward the listener, watch for the reaction of the listener, verify the message, ask for questions from the listener, and make a notation for follow-up if required.
- Proficient use of the telephone will reflect positively on your professional image. You should answer your own telephone whenever possible, try to return calls the same day, speak clearly into the telephone, leave messages indicating the best time to reach you, and avoid the use of cellular telephones in meetings.
- When giving an oral presentation, you should determine how much time you have for your presentation, select the best medium for delivery, identify key points you want to make, practice your presentation, be familiar with any equipment used, ask for feedback from someone in the group, and critique yourself.
- Your finesse in written communications is reflected in your ability to compose and deliver effective letters, e-mails, reports, and proposals.

- There are many occasions when you will want to express your appreciation to another professional for a courtesy. Some of these occasions include when he or she served as a reference for a job, gave you an opportunity to work on a project, provided assistance or advice, recommended you for a promotion, or gave you a gift.

- Listening is an important part of the communication process. You should develop your listening skills by giving your full attention to the speaker and following the message that is being communicated to you.

- It is important to learn the appropriate protocol for the internal communications of an organization.

- A professional respects the chain of command and follows it in internal communications.

- Communicating externally requires clarity and conciseness with customers with attention to timeliness and customer satisfaction.

- Remaining calm and focused during difficult situations will help distinguish you as a professional.

8
Professional Image Development

AT THE CORE
This topic examines:

➤ **MENTORS AND ROLE MODELS**
➤ **PUBLICATIONS**
➤ **TRAINING AND NETWORKING**
➤ **ASSESSMENT**
➤ **TAKING CRITICISM**

s a professional, you want to continue to learn and grow and to develop your professional image. Many sources can assist you in this development. A professional image is something you can develop and refine as you grow in your profession. Mentors, role models, publications, training, evaluations, and your own self-assessment can help you develop an objective view of yourself for professional development. It is important to recognize that all professionals continue to grow and develop as technology and situations change. Nancy Hancock Williams, management consultant and trainer, says, "Over the years, I've learned that forcing myself to acknowledge when I need to acquire new knowledge or skill has been one of the most important keys to my success in the business world."[1]

Mentors and Role Models

You will be fortunate if you are able to identify a mentor or role model who is willing to spend time with you and assist you in your professional development. Sometimes mentoring takes place on an informal basis and occurs without formal agreements. In some organizations, established mentoring programs exist. Inquiring about these during an interview is appropriate if you are interested in a formal mentoring program. Mentors can serve as role models for developing professionals. Many times a mentor will share informal or inside information that is difficult to learn as a new employee. However, this information can be invaluable to you. Mentors can share tips about the company and expected behavior and protocol for events and activities. Regardless of whether your organization has a formal mentoring program, you should identify some role models in your organization you can observe to determine how they dress, interact with others, complete their work, and support the work of the organization. You should always strive to develop yourself for a position of the future and not where you are today. Most people never "arrive" and consider their profession a journey to be enjoyed as they proceed through their career. Along the way, there are many people from whom you can learn. You can even learn things to avoid by observing situations and how people react to them. It is important to know what to do and what *not* to do.

In your interaction with a mentor or role model, you still must develop your own individual style and recognize the importance of your own decision making and the fulfillment of your individual responsibilities. What has been successful for one person may not be so for another. Assess your observations, and determine what may or may not be effective for you. This takes careful consideration and good judgment, which comes from experience. The final determination about your career rests on your abilities and expertise in your profession. Other people can be significant in your professional life, but the final determination lies in your efforts and abilities. Remember that you are ultimately responsible for your professional destiny.

> *"Real learning occurs after you think you know it all."*
> **—Florence Nightingale**

Publications

For the professional, numerous publications are available in both the traditional printed and electronic modes to help in the development of a professional image. This resource is readily available and affordable and can be reviewed at your convenience. You should make a habit of reading professional journals about your profession to maintain your knowledge level and to be aware of developing trends in your field. It is important to continue to learn. Journals, periodicals, online resources, and newsletters can offer information on a variety of topics and provide invaluable information about other resources. As with all resources, you must evaluate what information is appropriate and of value for your individual situation.

©PhotoDisc, Inc.

Training and Networking

Nothing is quite as valuable as training in your professional development. You can choose from a variety of training formats—from a short workshop or seminar of a few hours to a semester-long program of credit courses that are part of a formal educational program. You should have a professional development plan that includes goals and objectives for training in several aspects of your profession. You may work for an organization that is willing to provide tuition assistance for continuing your education and promoting your training opportunities. You should evaluate the content of an educational program to determine whether the cost of the training is worth your need for the information or expertise.

> *"Learn by doing. There is no substitute for experience and no finer teacher."*
>
> **—Mary-Ellen Drummond**

Other resources that can help in your professional development involve your interaction with other professionals in organizations and networks. You can learn a great deal about your profession and develop invaluable contacts by joining an organization where colleagues who share similar situations and challenges surround you in a professional environment. You can use these professionals as resources for problem solving and as role models. It helps to be surrounded by successful people who have already faced many of the issues you face. It can also be a great resource for career advancement. Therefore, you should project a professional image when surrounded by these individuals. Your organization may even support your involvement by contributing to your dues or allowing you to serve as an officer in an organization.

> *"You can't learn anything from experiences you're not having."*
>
> **—Louis L'Amour**

Assessment

Everyone is assessed at one time or another. Evaluation is part of your professional life and can be a positive aspect if you use it wisely. In most organizations, you have a preliminary period of probation after your initial hiring. You should use this time to learn as much as you can about your job and to interact positively with others so you can determine if the job is right for you. At the conclusion of your probation period, you can expect to meet with your supervisor to determine how well you are adjusting to the job, if there are any concerns, and how you can improve. You should view all job performance appraisals and evaluations as an opportunity to grow professionally. You will find that most supervisors want you to perform at a high level of proficiency— for your benefit and the organization's. The purpose of an evaluation is to provide feedback on how well your job performance is supporting the mission of the organization.

Another resource you have in assessing your performance is yourself. No one knows you as well as you know yourself; therefore, you should be a good judge of how you are doing in your career. However, you should have some established benchmarks for judging your success in your profession, as follows:

- Level of personal satisfaction in your position.
- Outcome of evaluations and appraisals given by supervisors.
- Progress toward financial security.

- Continuation of learning about your profession.
- Increase in job responsibilities and duties.
- Number of promotions and advancements made over a period of time.

All of these represent general areas of professional evaluation of your career and should tell you how well you are doing in your career over a period of time. The majority of these benchmarks should be positive if you want to be successful and satisfied in your profession.

Taking Criticism

At times in your career, you will be criticized for your performance or approach to a project or task. This can be another opportunity for professional growth if you learn from the experience. Criticism can come to you during an evaluation or appraisal or may be shared with you during an appointed time because of a situation. Try to avoid taking criticism as a personal attack; instead, consider it feedback on a job or task. Listen carefully to what is being said so you can determine how to correct the situation for the future. Look at the person who is speaking, and try to follow his or her thoughts as they are presented. When the person has finished his or her comments, you should ask questions and clarify what has been shared with you. Avoid making light of the situation or getting defensive about what was said. Most people need time to absorb what was shared with them so they can establish a plan of action to avoid the situation in the future. As a follow-up to criticism, you might ask for a meeting with the person to determine what course of action would have been more appropriate. In any event, it is usually to your advantage to take the criticism constructively and move beyond the present situation.

RECAP OF KEY CONCEPTS

- As a professional, you want to continue to learn and grow and develop your professional image as you proceed through your career.

- Mentors and role models can provide valuable guidance and information to assist you in the progression of your career and professional image development.

- Numerous publications are available to assist you in your professional image development. These include journals, periodicals, online resources, and newsletters.

- Training and networking are two valuable tools that can provide information on professional image development. Training should be an ongoing aspect of your professional development.

- Evaluation of your job performance is a normal aspect of your career. It is important to take job performance appraisals seriously and to learn from the information that is provided.

- Taking criticism constructively can be an opportunity for professional growth.

Case Studies

1. You have worked in your company for approximately five years and are familiar with the organization's mission. Your organization has grown substantially over the past few years, and many of the employees are actively involved with community activities. Management has expressed concern about the personal behavior of some individuals of the organization as they interact with the public. Because they represent the company in the public's eye, your company president has asked for the development of a code of behavior. You are a member of a cross-functional team that has been asked to compile a one-page code of personal behavior to be provided to all employees at the next professional development training session. Develop a code of behavior that is comprehensive, and addresses the critical areas of behavior for a professional. List below, in outline format, major headings and subheadings for the one-page handout.

2. You have been considering the development of a personal plan of action for the improvement of your professional image. Identify and list below six goals for improving your professional image. After listing the six goals, identify and list five action items that must be completed to move you toward the goal. Assign a timeline to each of the goals. Complete the activity by identifying all the resources available to help you accomplish these goals. Key this plan, and print a copy to remind yourself of your professional image goals.

_____

_____

_____

_____

_____

_____

_____

_____

_____

_____

_____

_____

_____

_____

3. Another competitor has recently purchased your company, and the anxiety about new management has been significant. Identify ten actions you can take to position yourself in a positive manner for the change of management. Prioritize these actions, and provide an explanation of why you believe each action item is important.

_____

_____

_____

_____

_____

_____

_____

_____

_____

_____

_____

_____

_____

_____

_____

_____

_____

4. You work for a relatively new company that markets pools and spas to the southeastern section of the country. Your primary customer is the homeowner who wants to improve his or her property and provide entertainment at home with the installation of a pool or spa. Your company has a relatively young sales team ranging in age from 20 to 40. You are responsible for one aspect of the training of the sales team members: communicating the importance of appropriate dress. Develop a set of guidelines for your sales team, so they know how to dress professionally and appropriately for their position.

_____

_____

_____

_____

_____

_____

_____

_____

_____

_____

_____

_____

_____

_____

_____

_____

Endnotes

Topic 1 – Professional Image

1. htttp://www.uwec.edu/Admin/Career/careerplanning/JobSearch/FAQ/18prodress.html
2. Ibid.
3. http://ecglink.com/newsletter/dressspk.html
4. Mary-Ellen Drummond, *A Woman's Way,* (Holbrook, MA: Adams Media Corporation, 2001), p. 75.

Topic 2 – Professional Appearance

1. Mary Mitchell, "Dress for Success: 9 Tips for Professional-Looking Hair," http://www.ivillage.com/work/job/succeed/articles/0,10109,165472_233366,00.html
2. A. Tariq Shakoor, "Dress to Impress," http://www.black-collegian.com/career/dressimpress1999-1st.shtml
3. Mary Spillane and Christine Sherlock, *Color Me Beautiful's Looking Your Best,* (Lanham, MD: Madison Books, 1995), p. 105.
4. Ibid., p. 97.
5. Ibid., p. 101.
6. Ibid., p. 159.
7. Caroline Reynolds, *Dimensions in Professional Development,* (South-Western Publishing Company, 1988) pp. 14-16.

Topic 3 – Professional Dress

1. Susan Bixler, *Professional Presence,* (New York: The Berkley Publishing Group, 1992) p. 141.
2. Jill Bremer, "Making Business Casual Work For You" (www.bremercommunications.com/Business_Casual.htm)
3. Bixler, p. 153.
4. Ibid., p. 158.
5. Ibid., p. 166.
6. Spillane and Sherlock, p. 132.
7. Ibid.
8. Tim Meehan, *Suit Yourself,* (USA, 1999) p. 2.
9. Ibid., p. 5.
10. Bixler, pp. 152-153.
11. Meehan, p. 39.
12. Ibid., p. 4.
13. Ibid., p. 37.
14. Lands' End, 2002 Spring Catalog, p. 3.

Topic 4 – Wardrobe Management

1. Spillane and Sherlock, pp. 73-79.
2. Meehan, p. 23.
3. Spillane and Sherlock, p. 90.
4. Reynolds, pp. 108-113.

Topic 5 – Manners and Etiquette for the Professional

1. Drummond, p. 82.
2. Ibid., p. 214.
3. Bixler, p. 37.
4. Drummond, p. 83.
5. Bixler, p. 37.
6. Ibid., p. 273.

Topic 6 – Personal Behavior

1. Ibid., p. 111.

Topic 7 – Communicating Professionally

1. Stephen R. Covey, *The 7 Habits of Highly Effective People,* (New York: Simon & Schuster, 1989), p. 236.

Topic 8 – Professional Image Development

1. Drummond, p. 83.

Online Resources

Professional Image
http://www.uwec.edu/Admin/Career/careerplanning/JobSearch/FAQ/
18prodress.html
This site discusses the importance of professional image.

http://ecglink.com/newsletter/dressspk.html
Dressing professionally is discussed at this site.

http://yourbestimagepid.com/
The site explains the relationship between a solid sense of self-confidence and looking and feeling good. The site includes some before and after photos.

http://www.jobfind.com/cc_feature_prof_image.htm
This site presents the concepts of nonverbal messages and how these relate to success.

Professional Appearance
http://www.ivillage.com/work/job/succeed/articles/
0,10109,165472_233366,00.html
This site offers a variety of topics and articles related to professional dress.

http://www.black-collegian.com/career/dressimpress1999-1st.shtml
This site shares tips on how to dress to impress in the professional environment.

Professional Dress
http://www.nccu.edu/business/pd/attire.htm
Guiding principles for the conservative-style wardrobe, which is appropriate for all corporate settings, are presented.

http://jobsearch.nmu.edu/students/articles/dress/m.pro.php
Professional business attire for men is discussed at this site.

Wardrobe Management
http://makinrent.tripod.com/image.index.html
This site discusses how to have a professional image on a budget.

http://ga.essortment.com/basicwardrobe_rblv.htm
The site explains how to put together a basic wardrobe even on a limited budget.

Manners and Etiquette for the Professional
http://www.rareinformation.com/ettiq.htm
This site explains why good manners mean good business.

http://www.netique.com/giftsearch/corpgift.html#anchor63097
The topic of gift giving and how it builds or maintains business relations is presented at this site.

http://www.epicurious.com/c_play/c02_polite/polite.html
Topics on eating in style and how to cope with food problems in public are provided at this site.

Personal Behavior
http://facetofacematters.com/pages/cnflttps.htm
Dealing with personal conflict in a professional manner is the focus of this site.

http://www.diversityinc.com/
This is an online magazine that provides news, resources, and commentary on the role of diversity.

Communicating Professionally
http://www.english.eku.edu/wisewords/
This site is devoted to helping you improve your skill in business communications.

http://www.sba.gov/gopher/Business-Development/Success-Series/Vol6/morale.txt
This site will motivate you to write letters of appreciation.

Professional Image Development
http://www.powerpointers.com/printarticle.asp?articleid=503
Tips on taking criticism are presented at this site.

http://www.careerbuilder.com/subcat/WLB/gwlb060111.html
This site will help you develop your networking skills.

Note: These Web sites were operational at the time of printing. However, since the Web is everchanging, specific URLs can change or expire very quickly. If you are unable to access these sites, use the following keywords to conduct an Internet search:

professional image
business image
wardrobe management
professional dress
casual dress
business attire
public speaking
business communications
ethics
diversity
business protocol
etiquette
business etiquette

Post-Assessment Activity

Directions: Read each of the following statements and questions carefully. Circle the letter of the best response.

1. Which of the following are attributes of a professional image?
   a. professional appearance
   b. use of manners and etiquette
   c. appropriate personal behavior
   d. effective communications
   e. all of the above

2. Being aware of which section of the country in which you reside as it relates to your professional dress means you are making decisions about your appearance based on which of the following criteria?
   a. types of functions you must attend
   b. geographic location
   c. budget and purchasing techniques
   d. clothing care and maintenance
   e. profession

3. A first impression is usually made within what time frame?
   a. 5 to 30 seconds
   b. 10 minutes
   c. after 15 minutes
   d. 30 minutes
   e. 1 hour

4. What is the major personal benefit of having a positive professional image?
   a. developing better friends
   b. being an effective communicator
   c. having a heightened sense of self-confidence
   d. having positive performance appraisals
   e. earning a better salary

5. What is an element of a healthy lifestyle as it relates to professional image?
   a. nutrition
   b. exercise
   c. diet
   d. regular visits to a physician
   e. all of the above

6. Characteristics of professional dress include:
   a. comfortable and casual
   b. comfortable and a proper fit
   c. well-maintained and clean
   d. appropriate for all occasions
   e. both b and c

7. What concept related to professional dress has developed over the past decade?
   a. company policies regarding dress
   b. uniforms for employees
   c. casual dress day
   d. customer profiling regarding dress
   e. none of the above

8. What color of a basic suit is best for the male professional?
   a. beige or khaki
   b. dark basic color such as charcoal gray
   c. navy blue
   d. black
   e. burgundy

9. What is the most powerful item of clothing for female professionals?
   a. skirted suit
   b. business dress
   c. jacket
   d. pantsuit
   e. briefcase

10. Lines that accentuate the body can be created by:
    a. a seam
    b. a hem
    c. color
    d. the end of a garment
    e. all of the above

11. How far below the hem of the sleeve of a suit jacket should a man's shirt sleeve extend?
    a. not at all
    b. one-half to three-quarters of an inch
    c. one inch
    d. less than one-quarter of an inch
    e. more than one inch

12. Hosiery should match which item for a woman?
    a. jacket
    b. skirt
    c. shoes
    d. blouse
    e. all of the above

13. What is the primary accessory for the male professional?
    a. tie
    b. belt
    c. shoes
    d. jewelry
    e. socks

14. Being respectful of another person's background and ethnicity is related to what concept?
    a. manners
    b. etiquette
    c. cultural diversity
    d. appreciation
    e. protocol

15. When introducing people, what is a good general rule to remember?
    a. make introductions during the first 15 seconds of people meeting
    b. mention first the name of the person you want to honor
    c. give a short introduction about the person prior to providing names
    d. let others introduce themselves
    e. ask if the people in the group know each other

16. When should you place your napkin in your lap at dinner in a restaurant?
    a. as soon as you are seated
    b. after the server takes drink orders
    c. prior to the first course
    d. when the salad is served
    e. when the host places the napkin in his or her lap

17. What should be the objective of giving a gift to someone who has extended a kindness to you?
    a. to show that you appreciate his or her kindness
    b. to demonstrate your good taste in gift selection
    c. to maintain a friendship
    d. to avoid any obligation on your part
    e. all of the above

18. Which characteristic is demonstrated by doing your job correctly in a timely manner without someone telling you to do it?
    a. initiative
    b. honesty
    c. integrity
    d. responsibility
    e. trustworthiness

19. What is one of the most difficult changes for professionals to accept?
    a. dress codes in their profession
    b. organizational structure in their company
    c. job relocations
    d. new policies
    e. performance appraisals

20. What type of communication is offensive to some people and difficult to understand?
    a. slang
    b. cursing
    c. acronyms
    d. jargon
    e. all of the above

Notes

Notes

Notes

Notes

Notes

Notes

Notes

Notes

Notes

Notes